OUR MISSION REVEALED

OUR MISSION REVEALED

AFSPPF

"THE UNIT THAT DIDN'T EXIST"

The true story and history of the Air Force Special Projects Production Facility

Lloyd R. Spanberger

To order additional copies of this book, contact:
Xlibris
1-888-795-4274
www.Xlibris.com
Orders@Xlibris.com
609387

CONTENTS

Dedication

Most all "Cold War" battle participants will never receive the respect and honor given those involved in conventional warfare activities because of the inherent differences between the two. However, these silent warriors possessed those qualities of "Duty", "Honor", and "Country" held in such esteem by all Americans. It is for these reasons this book is dedicated to those men and women who contributed to the mission of the Air Force Special Projects Production Facility (AFSPPF) and, by extension, to their spouses and families who had to endure the long hours and hardships imposed by the highly classified work involved.

ACKNOWLEDGEMENTS

I want to thank the many alumni who contributed to this historical rendering of our organization. Many personal discussions and several brainstorming sessions were held to establish the facts and recall the stories related to our experiences. Please see the appendices to learn of the many contributors and see a listing of those members who submitted a brief history of their involvement with the facility. This document could not have been written without their help and counsel. The reader is especially encouraged to read Appendix A for a biographical summary of major contributors, along with the author. The following individuals, however, have contributed immensely to the details herein and they deserve special thanks for their input. They are all good friends and were significant assets to our organization, during the time they served.

Alfred (Al) C. Crane: Al is a retired Lt Col, USAF who has spent several years researching the details of the facility's history and has assisted in reviewing the entire document several times prior to publishing, to verify its accuracy. He served as head of the Quality Control Division of the facility and ensured that only the best product possible came out. I remember the good times we had while serving together during those years. We have met privately many times to discuss the various aspects of our history and its presentation to our members and families, as well as to the public. He has also contributed to the design ideas leading to the establishment of our memorial plaque, now on display in The National Museum of the U.S. Air Force at Wright Patterson AFB, Dayton, Ohio.

James (Jim) O. Grimm: Jim is a retired CMSgt, USAF who had an extensive career dealing with the development and processing of military intelligence. He ran the photo-processing lab of our facility for many years. He has provided detailed insight into the operation of our laboratory and the many aspects of the day-to-day operation of our facility. We have had many discussions regarding our history and his personal experiences. His insight has contributed greatly to the content of this book. He has also served with the many organizations we were affiliated with during our existence, especially in overseas locations, and is most directly responsible for the quality of the many precision photographic processing labs throughout the Air Force, during his years of service.

Samuel (Sam) D. McCulloch: Sam is a retired Lt Col, USAF who served in the formative days of our facility. He has provided many insights into its early operation and has contributed many interesting stories of unusual events that took place back then. I have grown to respect his knowledge and integrity as a person and advisor to this document. He has filled in many gaps of knowledge, concerning our early days, and has provided insight into some of the political factors involved, during those times. Our original commander relied on him for extensive technical support during those formative years. Sam attended many meetings with him and NRO/CIA high-level officials.

Allen F. Ostdiek: Allen was an Air Force Captain and the officer in charge (OIC) of the Shipping Section of our facility from 1967 to 1971. He contributed to our brainstorming sessions and the majority of content in Chapter 5. He helped review this entire historical document, prior to publication. He was responsible for shipping finished product to our many customers and arranged the courier flights to accomplish this task. He also served as a courier on many of those flights. Be sure to read of his experiences in Chapter 5.

Definitions of Acronyms, abbreviations, etc. used throughout this book

24/7	----	Twenty four hours a day, seven days a week
A-12	----	Early Version of the SR-71 Spy Aircraft
AAF	----	Army Air Force
AFB	----	Air Force Base
AFOEA	----	Air Force Organizational Excellence Award
AFSC	----	Air Force System Command
AFSC	----	Air Force Specially Code
AFSPPF	----	Air Force Special Projects Production Facility
AFSPPL	----	Air Force Special Projects Production Laboratory
AFSPPL	----	Air Force Satellite Photographic Processing Laboratory
AIM	----	Aerial Image Modulation
ANG	----	Air National Guard
ARPA	----	Advanced Research Projects Agency
ASA	----	American Standards Association (Refers to photographic Film Speed)
ASD	----	Aeronautical Systems Division
ATRW	----	Aerospace Reconnaissance Technical Squadron
B-52	----	Air Force Bomber Aircraft
BDA	----	Bomb Damage Assessment
CCB	----	Configuration Control Board
CIA	----	Central Intelligence Agency
CMSgt	----	Chief Master Sergeant
Col	----	Colonel
CONUS	----	Continental United States
CORN	----	Controlled Range Network or Controlled Optical Range network
D-21	----	Supersonic Tagboard Drone
D-21B	----	Modified Version of the D-21 Tagboard Drone for Launch from a B-52
DARPA	----	Defense Advanced Research Projects Agency
DIA	----	Defense Intelligence Agency
DOD	----	Department of Defense
Dup	----	Duplicate
EK	----	Eastman Kodak Corporation
FLIR	----	Forward Looking Infrared

GOES	----	Geostationary Operational Environmental Satellite
GPS	----	Global Positioning Satellite
H&D curve	----	Graph showing Relationship Between Film Exposure & Image Density
HQ	----	Headquarters
IDA	----	Institute for Defense Analysis
IR	----	Infrared
KH	----	Keyhole : Name of the satellite reconnaissance security system
Lt Col	----	Lieutenant Colonel
M-21	----	YF-12 Mother Ship for the D-21 Tagboard Drone
MAC	----	Material Air Command
MAT	----	Material Air Transport
MIT	----	Massachusetts Institute of Technology
mm	----	Millimeters
MOL	----	Manned Orbiting Laboratory
MSgt	----	Master Sergeant
MTF	----	Modulation Transfer Function
NASA	----	National Air and Space Administration
NATO	----	North American Treaty Organization
NCO	----	Non Commissioned Officer
NCOIC	----	Non Commissioned Officer in Charge
NGA	----	National Geospatial-Intelligence Agency
NIMA	----	National Imagery and Mapping Agency
NOAA	----	National Oceanic and Atmospheric Administration
NPIC	----	National Photographic Interpretation Center
NRO	----	National Reconnaissance Organization
NRP	----	National Reconnaissance Program
NRTSC	----	Naval Reconnaissance Technical Support Center
O/N	----	Original Negative
O-6	----	Air Force Colonel
OIC	----	Officer In Charge
OPIC-A	----	Overseas Processing and Interpretation Center - Asia
OSAF	----	Office of the Secretary of the Air Force
PACAF	----	Pacific Air Forces - A major command of the US Air Force
PCS	----	Permanent Change of Station

PE	----	Perkin Elmer Corporation
PET	----	Performance Evaluation Team
QC	----	Quality Control
R&D	----	Research and Development
RADC	----	Rome Air Development Center
Recci-Tech	----	Reconnaissance Technical
RIT	----	Rochester Institute of Technology
ROKAF	----	Republic Of Korea Air Force
RTG	----	Reconnaissance Technical Group
RTS	----	Reconnaissance Technical Squadron
RW	----	Reconnaissance Warfare
SAC	----	Strategic Air Command
SAMSO	----	Space And Missile Systems Organization
SAO	----	Special Activities Office
SAR	----	Synthetic Aperture Radar
SG	----	Support Group
SMSgt	----	Senior Master Sergeant
SPIE	----	Society of Photographic and Instrumentation Engineers
SPO	----	System Project Office or System Program Office
SR-71	----	Super Sonic High Altitude Spy Aircraft
SRW	----	Strategic Reconnaissance Wing
SSgt	----	Staff Sergeant
TAC	----	Tactical Air Command
TDY	----	Temporary Duty
TEP	----	Transparent Electro Photographic
TIG	----	Tactical Intelligence Group
TS	----	Test Squadron
TSgt	----	Technical Sergeant
U-2	----	High Altitude Spy Aircraft (Sub Sonic)
UMD	----	Unit Manning Document
USAF	----	United States Air Force
USAFE	----	US Air Force Europe
USMCR	----	US Marine Corp Reserve
USN	----	United States Navy
WPAFB	----	Wright Patterson Air Force Base
X-15	----	Mach 5+ Rocket Plane
YF-12	----	Two Seat Version of the A-12

PREFACE

Back in the 1950's, the United States was in the midst of a Cold War with the Soviet Union. It is well known that President Eisenhower and his administration were seriously concerned about the Soviet arms buildup and what steps our country should take to counteract it. Our intelligence community had no way to verify what was going on in denied areas of their country.

What was desperately needed was overhead reconnaissance of denied Soviet territory, to assess their missile and aircraft inventory, among other things. This was no small task. During this period, President Eisenhower authorized development of the U-2 spy aircraft, which gave us our first look behind the Iron Curtain. This program had many of its own problems and when Francis Gary Powers was shot down, the U-2 project came to a grinding halt, at least temporarily.

Right on its heels, however, our country developed a top secret, supersonic aircraft now known as the SR-71. Although the Air Force SR-71 didn't become truly operational until early 1964 (First flight in late December, 1963), its predecessor, the CIA's A-12 was first flown in mid 1962 under the code name "Oxcart". It was developed by the Lockheed Corporation, at their Skunk Works facility in Burbank, California, as was the U-2 and SR-71 aircraft, and was tested and operated at the extremely top-secret facility at Groom Lake, Nevada, also known as Area 51. While these aircraft provided a significant amount of intelligence to our country, Eisenhower, earlier, decided to exploit the potential of Satellite Reconnaissance. This would provide us with an overhead capability that couldn't be challenged by antiaircraft missiles and provide us with intelligence information over denied Soviet territory, with no restrictions.

This decision led to the ultimate development of the Corona film return satellite, which provided our country with more data in its first successful mission, than all the previous U-2 aircraft combined. Not to say there weren't difficulties with this system. It turns out, the first dozen missions failed, for various reasons, but then success came and we were on our way to a long and lasting program of space reconnaissance that still exists today.

This story is about the Air Force Special Projects Production Facility (AFSPPF), which began its evolvement in the early 1960's. The facility was but a small part of the overall film return reconnaissance satellite program, but it played an extremely important roll. Its mission was, to conduct research and development (R&D) to provide the best equipment and techniques to support satellite photography and to produce, evaluate and distribute classified imagery from our nation's film return satellites and aerospace vehicles, with the highest possible quality. The information, contained herein, comes from the actual experiences of the people who did the work and served in this Air Force organization. Some information comes from documents recovered from official NRO and Air Force records, but the vast majority comes from firsthand knowledge of our alumni.

Although there is some amount of technical detail included in this history, it was not the intent to bore everyone with an abundance of it. The primary intent is to tell the story of our existence and our mission by relating the experiences of our people and our facility, which had to operate in a highly classified mode throughout our lifetime. Intense technical detail, about the satellites themselves, etc., may be found on the NRO web site and from other government sources, now that these programs have been declassified. There, you will find all the detail you can handle. Here, you will learn what it was like to live and work in an ultra Top Secret environment, while serving ones country. We worked hard, we had fun and now it's time to tell about it.

CHAPTER 1

Formation of the First Military Satellite Film Processing Laboratory

In late 1955, building P-1900 was built on Westover AFB, Chicopee Falls, Mass. Its purpose was to house the 8th Reconnaissance Technical Squadron (RTS). The 8th RTS was established as a Top Secret Strategic Air Command (SAC) unit, created to process and interpret classified reconnaissance imagery, produce target materials, and updated cartography for SAC. Figure 1 provides an aerial view of building P1900, whereas; figure 2 shows the front entrance of the building during the AFSPPF days.

Figure 1 Aerial view of building P1900, Westover AFB,
Chicopee Falls, Mass. (Early 1970's) (US Air Force Photo)

Figure 2 Front entrance view of building P1900, during the AFSPPF era
(US Air Force photo by Dick Wagner)

In mid December 1960, the Secretary of the Air Force established the AFSPPL (Air Force Satellite Photographic Processing Laboratory). It turns out the AFSPPL was a rename of the 6594th TS (Test Squadron), which was under the command of the 6594th Test Wing (Satellite). Subsequently, on or about 20 February 1961, the AFSPPL moved into Building P-1900 on Westover AFB. AFSPPL and the 8th RTS shared the building for a couple years before 8th RTS was moved to another location on base, after providing some resources and manning to the AFSPPL, whereby it continued its SAC mission. AFSPPL retained priority over all resources. Figures 3 & 4 show pages 1 & 2 of the original order issued by the Secretary of The Air Force.

CONFIDENTIAL

NO: 116.2
DATE: December 15, 1960

SECRETARY OF THE AIR FORCE
ORDER

SUBJECT: Organization and Functions of the Air Force
Satellite Photographic Processing Laboratory

1. There is hereby established the Air Force Satellite
Photographic Processing Laboratory (AFSPPL) at Westover Air
Force Base, Massachusetts.

2. The Laboratory will be under the command of the
Director of the SAMOS Project, 2400 East El Segundo Boulevard,
El Segundo, California. It will be attached to the Air Force
Command and Control Development Division, Air Research and
Development Command, L. G. Hanscom Field, Massachusetts, for
administrative, logistic, and contractual support.

3. The mission of the AFSPPL will be to conduct the
research and development necessary to provide the best possible
equipment, techniques, and knowledge applicable to satellite
photography, to insure that the processing and duplication of
photography obtained from satellite vehicles is of the highest
possible quality, and to process, duplicate, and distribute
this photography to designated users.

4. Physical space and some resources and manning for the
AFSPPL will be taken from the 8th Reconnaissance Technical
Squadron. The 8th Reconnaissance Technical Squadron will

SAFSR P.20

AFHQ FORM 0-968, 17 JUN 53

CONFIDENTIAL

Figure 3 (Page 1) of Secretary of the Air Force order establishing the
AFSPPL as the Satellite Photographic Processing Laboratory

CONFIDENTIAL

NO: 116.2
DATE: December 15, 1960

remain as a separate unit, with the AFSPPL having priority over all resources. Actual transfer of spaces, manpower, and other resources will follow approval of a detailed plan to be submitted to the Secretary of the Air Force by the Director of the SAMOS Project.

Dudley C. Sharp

CONFIDENTIAL

Figure 4 (Page 2) of the Secretary of the Air Force order establishing the AFSPPL

As can be seen in Figures 3 and 4, the AFSPPL was put under the command of the Director of the SAMOS Project, El Segundo, CA, which, in turn, reported directly to the Secretary of the Air Force. It was administratively attached to the Air Research and Development Command, L.G. Hanscom Field, Bedford, Massachusetts, for administrative, logistic and contractual support. AFSPPL was a tenant organization on Westover AFB. The base provided the first level of security for the facility, as well as housing, medical, recreational and general support services for the personnel. All personnel records were maintained at Hanscom Field. From this point on, Westover base personnel, of any nature, including SAC personnel had absolutely no access to Building P-1900.

The 6594th TS/AFSPPL was awarded the Air Force Outstanding Unit Award for period 01 May 1962 – 31 Dec 1963. It was during this period, in Oct 1962, when the facility processed U-2 intelligence imagery regarding the presence of Soviet Union missiles on Cuba. It is not clear how extensive this support was, but it is recalled that several of these U-2 missions were processed in the lab and promptly distributed to the intelligence community. Successful rapid precision processing and distribution of the U-2 imagery proved the outstanding competence of the facility. It must be noted that several other processing labs were utilized in the processing of U-2 missions during the Cuban missile crisis, as well. According to Strategic Air Command (SAC) historical Study No. 90 (Document number B-91816, Volume I, page 28), we were one of five organizations involved. SAC was in charge of U-2 operations during this time and controlled the handling of reconnaissance film from all missions. Our job was to take what we were given, process it and get it to the analysts in a timely manner, which is exactly what we did.

AFSPPL got a name change to Air Force Special Projects Production Laboratory (still AFSPPL) on 25 August 1964. This appears to be an attempt to hide the true purpose of the facility by eliminating the reference to satellites. The facility was then put under the command of the Director of Special Projects, OSAF (Office of the Secretary of the Air Force), in El Segundo, California. It was assigned organizationally to the 6594th Aerospace Test wing, AFSC (Air Force Systems Command), Sunnyvale, California. The stated mission was to conduct the R&D necessary to provide the best possible production equipment and techniques in support of special projects specified by the Secretary of the Air Force. At this point, R&D became a major activity of the organization, as well as the duplication, evaluation and distribution of satellite and aerospace imagery. See Figure 5 for the order relating to this change.

FOR OFFICIAL USE ONLY

NO: 116.3

DATE: August 25, 1964

SECRETARY OF THE AIR FORCE
ORDER

SUBJECT: Organization and Function of the Air Force Special Projects Production Laboratory

1. There is hereby established the Air Force Special Projects Production Laboratory (AFSPPL) (U) at Westover Air Force Base, Massachusetts.

2. The Laboratory will be under the command of the Director of Special Projects, OSAF, 2400 East El Segundo Boulevard, El Segundo, California. It will be assigned organizationally to the 6594th Aerospace Test Wing (AFSC), Sunnyvale, California. Host base will provide support in accordance with AFR 11-4.

3. The mission of the AFSPPL will be to conduct the research and development necessary to provide the best possible production equipment and techniques in support of special projects specified by the Secretary of the Air Force.

EUGENE M. ZUCKERT
Secretary of the Air Force

AFHQ FORM 0-861, 17 JUN 81

FOR OFFICIAL USE ONLY

Figure 5 Secretary of the Air Force order re-establishing AFSPPL as the Special Projects Production Laboratory

The final name change to Air Force Special Projects Production Facility (AFSPPF) came on or about 10 November 1965. The stated mission, however, remained the same. The facility was then assigned to the Air Force Systems Command and then further assigned to the Space Systems Command. On or about 01 July 1967, the organization was assigned to the Space and Missile Systems Organization (SAMSO).

Note: Figures 3-5 are cleaned up copies of the original NRO copies shown in Appendix C. These and other NRO documents may be found on the NRO web site. Copies of all documents shown in Appendix C were obtained from the NRO web site.

Throughout all these name changes and organization assignments, the facility was under the direction of the National Reconnaissance Organization (NRO), which was a classified organization in itself, and the CIA. This final name change was apparently made in a last ditch attempt to mask the true mission of the organization, by eliminating any reference to photography, satellites, or a laboratory. We were now just a facility doing special projects, whatever that meant.

Documented history?

There is no declassified documented record of the personnel breakdown of any organization occupying building P-1900. Where copies of official documents could be obtained, they are presented herein (See Appendix C).

The estimated breakdowns presented in this history come from the officers, NCOs and enlisted men, still around after all these years. Multiple brainstorming sessions were held during our reunion in Branson, MO, in October 2012, whereby details of our history were recalled and verified by former members of these various organizations.

All total, there were approximately twelve hours or more of time spent in these sessions. Everyone present did their best to remember and contribute their experiences, while serving in our organization and the various organizations with which we were associated. It seemed that the more we talked the more we were able to remember. This, of course, was the purpose of these sessions and it worked well. All sessions were recorded to provide an audio backup of the information gleaned from the well-seasoned minds of our attendees. One final session was held during our reunion in September 2013, during which a preliminary document was reviewed and commented on by many of our members. This resulted in more information and stories being added along with the making of several refinements. This session was recorded, as well.

The following two photos show the brainstorming sessions held during our 2012 reunion.

AFSPPF Brainstorming crew posing (Photo by James E. McLaurin)

Front row left to right: Bob Sisson, Jim Grimm, Mike Riley, Lloyd Spanberger, Hal Gordon, Tom Shacklett, Allen Ostdiek

Back row left to right: Herb Duval, Russ Sanner, Leroy (Moose) Miller, Sam McCulloch, George White, Lee Colville

Not Pictured, but participating, was Leman (Mac) McBrayer.

AFSPPF Brainstorming crew working (Photo by James E. McLaurin)

From left to right around the table: Hal Gordon, Herb Duval, Jim Grimm, Dick Temple (standing), Bill Ray, Bob Sisson, Erich Kassler (standing), Mike Riley, Allen Ostdiek (standing), Lou Falconieri, Lloyd Spanberger, Sam McCulloch

Not Pictured, but participating, was Leman (Mac) McBrayer.

Location, Location, Location

Location of the facility was also important. Political policy decisions and Cold War activities were based on the most advanced science and engineering developments in space satellite imaging technology, and therefore the facility's location on Westover AFB provided easy access to the Pentagon, academic institutions and industrial corporations, who were Corona satellite pioneers, and could provide us with advanced technical support. Most scientific and engineering assistance was located in the Northeast sector of the United States, a few hours driving distance from the facility. Educational institutions and corporations included Rochester Institute of Technology (RIT), Massachusetts Institute of Technology (MIT), Eastman Kodak, Itek Corporation, Perkin Elmer and Technical Operations Corporation. Lowry AFB Technical Training Center, NRO, CIA, DOD and Air Force Systems Command were government-supporting organizations.

Yes, this sounds very confusing, and maybe that was the purpose of it all. In actuality, very little of all this made any difference to those of us who worked there. We just did our jobs and got things done. Having direction and support from the top levels of our government, made life a lot easier when it came to getting the personnel, equipment and the resources we needed and there seemed to be no limit to our travel budget. Of course, we were still in the military, so our per diem for travel was a bit subpar, to say the least. We always had to find the lowest cost accommodations, etc. Our civilian counterparts were much better off. Not only did they receive triple our pay, or more, but they had a much better per diem plan. They could afford quality motels and got a better choice of food. Such was our life back then.

Today's world

Electro-optical techniques dominate classified reconnaissance in today's world, so there is no longer a reason to deal with sophisticated film-handling problems, except, perhaps, in specialized cases. Clean rooms, climate controlled computer rooms! Who needs them any longer! Desktops, laptops, I-pads, I-pods, I-everything have taken over and everyone has them at relatively low cost.

Photographic film is all but gone, replaced by electronic digital cameras with megapixel sensors in the civilian world and gigapixel sensor arrays in the military and certain commercial enterprises. Since the images are now digitized, they can be manipulated with computer software, giving the interpreters a vast array of options never possible with the old film processing methods.

Computer hacking seems to be the big problem with security today, but back then, hacking had more to do with hatchets and saws. Things do change over time. We had locked doors made of steel, etc. Today we have firewalls made of bits and bytes. What is this world coming to? Large-scale precision film processing technology has now gone the way of the 'buggy whip' and the 'slide rule'. The skills needed back then are no longer in demand, in today's military and civilian marketplace.

Real time reconnaissance was a dream back then but is reality today, along with a fair degree of real time and automated analysis, envied by us old timers. Greater things are coming in the future, as it always does. Looking back provides a certain amount of perspective and appreciation of the challenges encountered and overcome. In the future, today's generation will look back and wonder how they managed to survive with the ancient technology we have today. They will live in a real time communication world we cannot even imagine at this time. I have no doubt that signal processing techniques and machines that do our thinking for us will become extremely powerful. Watch out for those annoying robots. At least they probably won't eat, we hope. On second thought, we are making some of our gas from corn these days and, since gas is used to produce some amount of electricity in use by today's fledgling robots, I guess they are already eating our food. Don't say you weren't warned!

People working in today's environment have no concept of what had to be done to provide the high quality product needed by our intelligence community back in the, so called, "good old days". Great credit is due to all those military members who made it all happen with long hours, low pay and very little recognition for their efforts. Here's hoping this document will provide a level of insight into our accomplishments and those of you who served in our facility or its associated organizations will, some day, be appreciated for your contributions.

The day before yesterday's world of military photo processing

Photoreconnaissance has been around for quite a long time, as can be seen by the following photographs. I'm sure one can easily tell that these were the really really good old days. I, for one, however, am very happy to have not had to put up with their working conditions, except, perhaps, for the lack of hair cut and shiny shoes requirements. I wonder what their "happy hours" were like.

Civil war mobile photographic dark room

Civil war high tech photographic technicians

Now, these guys were true pioneers in the art of photographic film processing. I'm willing to bet they didn't even have slide rules to work with, yet, they got the job done. Would someone please point out where the clean room is in these pictures and why are they not wearing bunny suits? Have we come a long way baby, or what? I wanted to get permission to use their photos, but I just couldn't find them. I hope they don't mind going down in history, along with you all. I hope this provides just a bit of perspective. Oh yea, by the way, I don't see them wearing security badges either. What's that all about?

I am also willing to bet they had no concept of aerial or satellite reconnaissance. There was no way they could have conceived of such things back then. Thoughts of that nature were reserved for science fiction writers alone. Thinking about all that makes one realize why we couldn't conceive of the memory capacity and power of the digital cameras we have today. All this high technology had to develop a little bit at a time back then, but today it's developing at a geometric rate, which makes it all the more difficult to forecast the future, beyond a few years.

What does the future hold?

Obviously, we have no idea, but we can have fun speculating.

Our cell phones and GPS devices are now talking to us and eventually they will start to ask why we don't pay more attention to them. Soon, these little devices will be able to tap the power of full-blown super computers, as well as the internet. I can even visualize neural implants that will allow instant communications with everyone without even having to push buttons or turning power on. Hmmm, will we be able to turn these things off? I'm sure every teen-age girl in the world will want this capability (ok, some of the guys will too). Batteries won't even be required, since these devices will probably have their own built in generators, powered, in some way, by our internal organs. Imagine charging our internal batteries by eating junk food. How good can it get?

It could be great for us old timers too. Imagine built in medical alert functions and perhaps cyber doctors getting readouts of our condition, telling us what to do, transmitting instant cures or dispatching immediate help, and all this without using a phone. Planning trips, scheduling transportation, making dinner reservations, paying bills or whatever, will happen in a flash. Perhaps images could be transmitted directly to our brains, eliminating the need for cell phone or lap top screens. Will 3D printing become the forerunner of a transporter device? Star Trek, here we come.

This could all be relative good news, but what about the bad news. Will your privacy disappear, will organized crime take advantage of this technology (after all, they have all the money) and could you lose control of your life. Could the bad guys hack you and whack you by zapping you? These are simply questions and food for thought for the next generation. For that future generation, today is the day before yesterday. However, just as those early pioneers pictured above, it's not our problem. It's just fun to think and wonder about it. Let's let our grandkids worry about it, we have enough on our minds. By the way, what's for dinner tonight?

CHAPTER 2

"We Didn't Exist"

It was one thing to get film back from a satellite, all in one piece, but once it was retrieved, it had to be processed, duplicated and distributed to the intelligence community in a timely manner. Equally important was the need to extract the maximum amount of intelligence and make it visible to the human eye, for interpretation and analysis by CIA personnel and the US military.

Due to the sensitive mission of the AFSPPF, it, basically, didn't exist. Although it was physically located on Westover Air Force Base, near Springfield, MA, in a little town called Chicopee Falls, all personnel records were held ninety miles away, at Hanscom Field, in Bedford, MA. There were no indications of the actual mission of the unit. It was a tenant organization on the base and access was severely restricted. As an example, should a fire occur within the facility, AFSPPF personnel had the responsibility for inside response. Base firefighters would only be allowed inside, to assist, with escorts and added security. Fortunately, the situation never occurred.

Our first commander, Colonel Harold Z. Ohlmeyer, was very into sports competition on base and, as a result, we won many trophies. Often, when we were asked, by outside people, what we did in the facility, we would respond by telling them the building was a huge gymnasium where we practiced all day long. It was no wonder we won all those awards. There were no windows, so no one could see how we did it. This usually shut down the conversation. There was method in the Colonels madness, however. Focusing on sports took away from the intensity of the job. It helped a great deal in keeping up morale and maintaining a winning attitude, especially during long grueling missions. Our organization couldn't be publicly recognized for our work, but could be publicly recognized for our achievements on the ball fields.

Being non-existent certainly did not help in the area of personal recognition either. As an example, the Air Force Missleman Badge (Pocket Rocket) was awarded to Officers and Airmen that performed operational launch and maintenance duties with both strategic and tactical missiles. In addition, personnel assigned to research and development programs directly associated with missile technology (such as the Air Force Rocket Propulsion laboratory, Edwards AFB, CA) were also awarded the badge. Military personnel, assigned to the NRO Staff in Los Angeles and Washington D.C., were also qualified for the award and wearing of the "Pocket Rocket". However, apparently due to security concerns, no personnel assigned to the 6594th Test Squadron or the Air Force Special Projects Production Facility could be submitted for the award. They were denied formal, public recognition for their direct involvement in Space Based Reconnaissance Systems. Security, simply, had its downside when it came to personal recognition. If you did not get it before or after serving in AFSPPF, you just did not get it. This unit provided our country with the best photographic intelligence possible and as invisible as we were, we were still awarded the Air Force Organizational Excellence Award (AFOEA) for the periods:

01 Jul 1971 – 30 Jun 1972
01 Jul 1974 – 30 Jun 1976

At least the unit gained a little outside recognition, even though the individuals didn't.

Our personnel make-up consisted of approximately 28 civilians, 28 officers and 280 enlisted, of which about 28 were senior non commissioned officers (NCOs). What's with the number "28"? Is there something going on here that we still don't know anything about?

Pretty much everyone in the facility was handpicked, based on their experience and talents. Everyone had to go through an expanded background investigation, as well, due to the classified nature of the job. Several enlisted personnel worked part time at local banks, to make extra money. Having top-secret clearances were a serious asset for them, in the bank manager's eyes. It was at least one indication that our people could be trusted.

Although we had a social life outside the base, etc., we primarily hung out with our co-workers. The classified nature of our work was never discussed outside the facility, including with our spouses. If a slip up did occur, it was pretty much within the group and, therefore, no serious harm done. There was one particular situation, however, where someone, outside our ranks, kept showing up at our off base functions, such as in the bowling alley, coffee get-togethers, various parties, etc. It became almost obvious he was trying to find out what we were all about. He was eventually reported to our security officer and soon after, we had no further problem (Yea, I'm the one who turned him in). We learned later, that he worked for the Wall Street Journal, as a field agent. Who knows, maybe he lost his job, but he got no information from us and disappeared from the scene very quickly. I'm guessing it didn't pay to mess with our security.

On-base social activities usually consisted of occasional happy hours and frequent attendance at $2.00 steak night at the service clubs. These were fun times and we took advantage of them, when possible. As a result, we all got to know each other very well and those friendships still exist today.

Security became a way of life

Our facility used the base for normal housing, commissary, medical and recreation support. The base, of course, also provided the first level of security. The facility, itself, provided armed guard security within its walls, as well as cipher and combination locked vaulted rooms within. When one looks at the big picture, the information contained in the imagery delivered to our facility represented the result of billions of dollars spent in getting it there. The intelligence contained therein was virtually priceless. Security, therefore, was of the utmost importance for both financial and intelligence reasons. Everyone working within the facility needed a Top Secret, Talent Keyhole clearance, as a minimum. Byeman level clearances were held by a select few, on a need to know basis only. The Byeman clearances were directly related to the actual satellites themselves. As will be described later, these satellites included Samos, Corona, Gambit, Dorian and Hexagon. Special Crypto clearances were held by those responsible for secure, covert communications with the NRO, CIA and our customers, for a variety of reasons, including courier missions.

The building was secured by armed guards on a 24-7 basis. Upon entering the building, assigned personnel had to relinquish their ID badges for special inside use only badges. These badges indicated special areas inside the building, where they had access. The building itself, was a series of vault rooms, each having a cipher or combination lock at the entry points. One needed a specific project clearance for each category of rooms.

The only windows in the building were in the general administration areas, which included the commander's office and unclassified conference room.

As the years went on, the building became somewhat self-sufficient. By the mid 1960's it even had its own backup power generators, which would automatically kick in and provide essential support, if outside power was lost. The big Northeast Blackout of 1965 had no effect on our facility, what so ever, although we are now not sure exactly what happened. Either our own generators kicked in or we got power from the local town (Holyoke, MA), which had their own power generators.

By the end of 1970, the facility's backup power source received an upgrade by the installation of three large diesel generators. These generators came from the Titan Missile Site 5A, at Lowry AFB, closed down by SAC. MSgt Jack Anderson, the former NCOIC of that site's power plant, began his assignment to our facility in 1970 and wound up in charge of those same generators. Strange things do happen, or perhaps it was all part of the plan. We will never know, but then again, everyone assigned to the facility was handpicked. I am sure many of us would like to know who did the picking. Then again, perhaps some questions are best left unanswered.

Security was enhanced with motion detectors installed in the heating and ventilation ducts. Processed and titled film, ready for distribution, was transported to the shipping area via an underground conveyor system. Occasionally a rodent would get into the underground system, during down time, and set off the alarm. This was obviously a nuisance, and to this day, it's doubtful if the problem ever got solved. Who knows, those mice might have been enemy secret agents in disguise. Fortunately, back then, the technology wouldn't support such clandestine methods, but today it may be an entirely different matter.

Distribution

The finished product was distributed to intelligence customers, via armed courier service, which typically consisted of one officer or senior NCO and one additional enlisted person from the facility. Although there were times when air transportation was provided by other branches of the military, typically, the material was loaded onto a USAF cargo plane, by facility personnel, and flown to the various customers around the country. Delivery to the standard customer base was typically known as operation 'MINIBALL'.

Armed personnel never lost sight of any classified material until every item was delivered to its designated destination. Often times these missions lasted all night long and the couriers didn't get back home till the wee hours of the morning. In the early years, however, delivery sometimes took several days and couriers were occasionally left stranded at the last delivery site and had to find their own way back to Westover AFB. These were definitely not fun times.

Many times the plane would land and taxi to a remote area of a base, whereby a van would approach and, with the proper passwords, accept their share of material on board. The plane would then take off and head to its next destination. This process continued until the mission was complete. The pilots and normal crew were rarely allowed in the back of the plane, where the classified material was loaded. Their job was simply to get us to our drop off points on schedule. For the most part, they always did as they were instructed and we all got along just fine. Relationships between facility couriers and aircraft crews were perhaps a bit boring, but that was just the way we liked it. Fortunately, they had a military mind set, as did we. Although there were a few tense moments at times, this was definitely not like an adventure movie, where someone always screwed up by going their own way and breaking the rules. Some of these tense moments are described later on. Be on the lookout! They were quite interesting and could have been a bit messy, to say the least.

Bridgehead

When discussing the processing of satellite imagery, one must recognize the covert Bridgehead facility located in the Hawkeye Works of Eastman Kodak Company in Rochester, NY. This facility, under contract to the CIA, was initially created in 1955 to support the processing and duplication of Top Secret photographic film from Spy Aircraft and, later on, Film Return Satellites. AFSPPF worked very closely with the people at Bridgehead. We were duplicate facilities and much of our equipment came from them. They manufactured the actual film used for satellite reconnaissance and, of course, had the responsibility of developing the original negatives from satellite missions, as well as duplicate positives for certain customers. They will be mentioned now and then throughout this document, regarding their contributions and associations with our facility. The major difference between us is that we were military and they were civilian. Their people were paid much more than we were. We understood and accepted all that with no hard feelings (well, there may have been a little grumbling now and then). We were proud of what we did and knew the importance of our mission. We must admit, however, that the majority of the people working in both facilities knew little of what occurred in the other, due to the intense security restrictions in both. Many people in both facilities most likely had no idea the other even existed. Upon leaving the service, many of our personnel went to work for Kodak at the Bridgehead facility.

Since security was much the same, their spouses and family members also had no clue what they did, until recently. The Kodak people wrote up their history of Bridgehead, primarily for their own use and distribution, which now allows their friends and families to know of their contributions and accomplishments. We happen to have a copy of that history for reference and safekeeping. Their document gives brief mention of our facility, as though we were only a backup to theirs. It can only be surmised that the writers had only limited knowledge of our actual mission. The fact is, we were a backup for the processing of original negative imagery and we were ready to assume that additional responsibility, if it became necessary. Overall, however, we had a great cooperative working relationship with their people and many of them were good friends to the end. We thank them for their contribution to the efforts we were both engaged in.

CHAPTER 3

As the End Drew Near

As mentioned earlier, the stated mission of the AFSPPL was carried forward to the AFSPPF, all the way through to 1976. All in all, the organization in Building P-1900 was in operation from February 1961 through December 1976. It started with the 6594th Test Squadron, then AFSPPL (Twice) and finally AFSPPF for the duration of its mission.

On 01 January 1977, most of the equipment and several personnel were transferred to the 544th Aerospace Reconnaissance Technical Wing (ARTW) at HQ SAC, Offutt Air Force Base near Omaha, Nebraska. Some of the production processing equipment was possibly sent to the covert Bridgehead Lab at Eastman Kodak, in Rochester, NY. One of our key people (CMSgt Thomas S. Shacklett, Jr.) was transferred to Omaha (two years prior to our closure) to supervise and oversee the two million dollar overhaul of the photographic processing laboratory at the 544th ARTW, to continue the AFSPPF mission. He recalls that the duplication laboratory there was configured to become a viscous processing operation (It is believed Kodak was the primary mover to institute this process, since they tried to get it installed to do dual gamma duplicate processing at Westover in the early 1970's). This capability transfer had to be completed prior to the actual closure of AFSPPF. It was accomplished ahead of time and under budget. According to Tom, the 544th customers were limited to foreign locations and the approximately 40 AFSPPF domestic customers were then serviced by Kodak, from their Bridgehead facility.

Viscous duplicate processing was not done at the AFSPPF, since it was a complex and somewhat toxic process and produced no better results than the wet chemical spray process used throughout the entire history

---

of the facility. Original negative processing equipment, however, was converted to viscous to emulate the Kodak Bridgehead capability, should AFSPPF became tasked to produce original negative satellite imagery. Disposal of waste viscous material was very difficult and costly, compared to wet chemicals. Dual gamma duplicate processing was developed and implemented by AFSPPF personnel using normal wet spray processing techniques, without the expense of a viscous process. This saved the Air Force many millions of dollars, at the time. It was military personnel, in the facility, who developed the techniques to accomplish this mission, which greatly enhanced the quality of the finished product. Of course, since we didn't exist and our individual accomplishments couldn't be documented, little, if any, credit was given.

It is believed the evaluation function and associated equipment was moved to the National Photographic Interpretation Center (NPIC) in Washington DC. NPIC was renamed NIMA (National Imagery and Mapping Agency) and has since been finally renamed NGA (National Geospatial-Intelligence Agency), as of today. Throughout these changes, other intelligence activities were merged in. Who knows what now lies under the final NGA umbrella. It is further understood that the R&D projects were moved to the Office of Development and Engineering (OD&E), in an undisclosed location in the Washington DC area (Possibly the NRO). Westover AFB, itself, was being closed down and our facility would no longer have base security and adequate services to support it. It was a sad day for the people who were there at the end. The Gambit and Hexagon satellites were in full swing, at this point in time, and the existence of our facility was now lost forever. As of today, building P-1900, itself, no longer exists. See appendix C for copies of documents alluding to the disposition of our facility.

CHAPTER 4

What Went on Inside

The following organizational chart was put together from what little documentation we could gather and the personal recollections of our various remaining members.

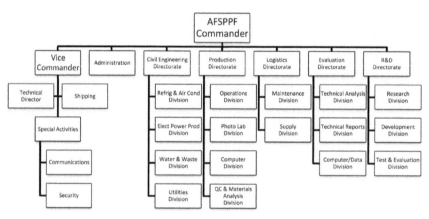

AFSPPF Organizational Chart

The five major operations within AFSPPF were the Civil Engineering, Production (Photo Lab & Quality Control (QC)), Logistics, Evaluation and Research and Development (R&D) Directorates. As previously mentioned, the unit was manned by, approximately, 28 officers, 28 civilians and 280 enlisted personnel, including 28 (14 Senior) NCOs. There's that pesky number 28 again. Even the number "14" is related to "28", like half.

Military physicists were assigned to QC and R&D. Everyone assigned to the operation was handpicked for their unique abilities and dedication to their jobs. Security was of the utmost importance and everyone treated it as such. There were no security leaks, at any time, throughout our history. Shipping and Special Activities, including Communications and Security, came under the Vice Commander.

An internal divisional breakdown was not attempted, due to the complexity of the various functions involved and the interaction between the various groups within each division. If something needed to get done, it didn't matter who said to do what. It was ok to help across division lines and we didn't always have to ask our immediate supervisors for permission. On a personal note, I often took assignments directly from the Commander, Vice Commander, Technical Director and the R&D Director (the directorate I was assigned to). I also supported the Production and Evaluation Directorate, without the need of a direct assignment. It all seems a bit complicated now but at the time, it was a normal situation. It was certainly a way to keep busy and the variety of activity was a lot of fun, as well. I believe a lot of us were in this situation.

Production Directorate

Photo Lab Division

Film processing and duplication was run in a clean room environment, under positive pressure, in order to keep any dust or contaminants out. The lab was illuminated with low-level red light and, since the duplicate positive film used was not sensitive to red light, personnel could work with at least some degree of visibility. The images contained in the final product had to be viewed on special film viewers, light tables or with microscopes. The images had to be expanded up to 10 to 20 times, or more, in order to see the detail buried within them. A speck of dust could potentially cover up an aircraft carrier, which was an unacceptable situation. State of the art high-speed printers and spray processors were used extensively in the operation. Calibration strips were periodically run through the process, in order to assure the proper chemical mix was in place to provide the correct quality for the mission. The lab ran 24 hours a day during a mission, until all duplicates were produced and distributed, via armed courier, to the entire intelligence community for strategic and tactical analysis. This lab was the largest clean room facility dedicated to classified film processing. Details of Lab operations will appear later in Chapter 8.

SPPL-1 & SPPL-2

Chemical formulas used for the production of duplicate film products (SPPL-1 & SPPL-2) were developed by the unit and approved for use by the National Reconnaissance Community. No contractor-prepackaged chemicals were used for the production of duplicate roll film products. Chemicals of photographic quality were procured in bulk and mixed for each mission. The Chemical mix facility was an expansive farm of stainless steel mixing & storage tanks, control monitors, distribution pumps and supply lines to the processing laboratory. Each batch of bulk chemicals was checked for purity and content by the unit's state of the art chemical analysis laboratory. Approximately 2-3 of the enlisted personnel, assigned to this function, were graduate chemists with either bachelor or masters degrees in the 99127 "Scientific Aide" AFSC that was awarded to them.

During the Cold War and Vietnam War, many people with college degrees did not qualify for commissions in the USAF due to quotas, etc. Recognizing the fact that the AF needed qualified scientists in the rapidly expanded R&D Laboratories and related activities, they instituted the AFSC 99127 ("Scientific Aide") category to take advantage of qualified scientists that could be put to immediate use in supporting vital national R&D programs. The 6594th TS/AFSPPF obtained authorization to have these limited billets added to their UMD (Unit Manning Document). These personnel received the same extensive background checks and scrutiny that was applied to all personnel being considered for the unit. Their enlistment was limited to one tour, but they were afforded the opportunity to compete for promotion, with their peers.

Exposure to Photographic Chemicals

Long-term exposure to photographic chemicals can be hazardous. While personnel assigned to chemical mix and those involved in the processing of the actual missions wore protective masks, to reduce particulate contamination, these items were not meant to provide protection for chemical dust or vapors in these rooms. Personnel were exposed, throughout their 12-hour shifts that lasted from 1-3 weeks at a time, depending on the mission. Although not typical, it was recalled that the longest mission was about two months long. In addition, personnel in the select enlargement lab, using Beacon Enlargers, were exposed to Trichloroethene used as a cleaning agent in the film/lens area. Unfortunately, very little consideration was given to the long-term effects of this kind of exposure. To this day, we have no idea if anyone developed problems from exposure and it is doubtful if we ever will know. Let's hope not.

Quality Control (QC) Division

QC made sure all duplicates were uniform so that image analysts all saw the same thing and could effectively communicate with each other, regarding target analysis. They routinely worked in close contact with Production to ensure the processing parameters were consistent throughout an entire mission run. QC pretty much served as the watchdog of the mission. No defects or low quality product got by their prying eyes. They ran a full chemical analysis laboratory and monitored the film processors to certify the proper chemical mix was established, at all times. Nothing was left to chance. Once the product got past QC, each frame was titled (frame ID, security level, etc.), if necessary, and sent to shipping where it was packaged for distribution.

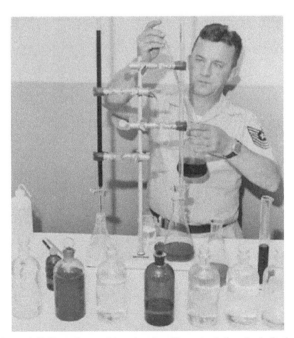

MSgt Joseph J. Paszik working in the Chemical Analysis Laboratory
(US Air Force Photo by Dick Wagner)

AFSPPF Chem Analysis Lab (US Air Force Photo)

Evaluation Directorate

The Evaluation Directorate analyzed the final product to determine overall mission quality. They used edge scanning and resolution target images (CORN targets, described later), within the mission photography, to score the detailed results of the mission. They compared the actual mission resolution to the ability of the film to record it, in order to determine the mission score. This process was a bit complex, but very effective, once perfected. Briefly, a MTF (modulation transfer function) curve was calculated from edge scans of the imagery (Camera performance) and was then compared to an Aerial Image Modulation (AIM) curve (Film capability). The intercept of the two curves was one measure of mission performance. An IBM 360 computer was used to create the resulting curves. At one point, R&D assisted in refining this process, which smoothed out the curves and eliminated false intercepts. Yes, the various groups actually worked with each other to constantly improve the quality of the missions. How radical can one get!

The following two photos, showing the IBM 360 and the supporting computer room, was located in an environmentally controlled room with a raised floor (all the interconnecting cabling was under the floor), which was a standard configuration back then. It is interesting to note that all this computer equipment could now be replaced by one smart cell phone today.

AFSPPF IBM 360 Computer (US Air Force Photo)

AFSPPF Computer Room (US Air Force Photo)

They, along with members of the intelligence community, namely the CIA, prepared a performance evaluation report, for every mission, which was used to identify and correct problems with the satellite camera systems and determine incentive rewards for the various contractors supporting the mission. This team of people was called the PET team (Performance Evaluation Team). The PET team was convened and hosted by our facility and headed by a representative from CIA headquarters (Langley, VA) for the majority of the missions. Once the mission was in-house, there was a 24-hour deadline (from the time Dup Positives were available from the lab) to evaluate it and produce a hard copy report of results.

CORN refers to a program named Controlled Range Network (sometimes called Controlled Optical Range Network). It consisted of a network of fixed and portable resolution targets. The portable targets would be deployed for a brief moment, as the satellites passed overhead. They would then be dismantled or gathered up. Our satellites were the only ones that would ever see them. As a side note, in order to provide a greater degree of flexibility, CORN targets were also painted on the top of the wings of certain RB-47 and RB-57 aircraft which, at times, were flown to certain locations, at certain altitudes, at just the right times, in the CONUS (Continental United States). Of course, the pilots had no idea why they were doing that. They just did as told. These aircraft were primarily stationed and flown out of Wright Patterson AFB (WPAFB). Prior to my assignment to the R&D Directorate at the facility and while stationed, as a research physicist, in the Infrared Reconnaissance Lab at WPAFB, I often flew on one of these RB-47 aircraft. At that time, I had no idea why it had test targets painted on its wings and little did I know what was in store for me in the future.

PET team makeup and goals

The PET team was typically made up as follows; two CIA representatives (one of which always chaired the meetings), two Air Force engineers from the west coast satellite operations center in Sunnyvale, CA (studying satellite performance) and representatives from the Camera contractors (Itek, Kodak or Perkin Elmer, where appropriate). They would arrive at our facility just prior to the first duplicates coming out of the lab. At first, they would meet privately to discuss the purpose of the mission and mission goals such as resolution vs. altitude, etc.

Independently, our people would begin to analyze the imagery regarding weather, slant angles, cloud cover, etc. We made all the decisions regarding how the data was obtained, although one of the west coast Air Force officers would occasionally suggest targets to scan based on viewing lab results, as they became available. The team was in constant contact with the lab throughout this first 24-hour period. There were times when primary focus of analysis was dictated by certain hot spots of activity in the world. These areas were determined by the team leader. We would also do a comparison analysis with previous missions and bring up significant variations to the team leader. We would provide derived data to the team, who would then run their own computer analysis, using their own software on our computer (IBM 360). Images of U.S. deployed CORN targets were used to determine resolution, etc. These targets were of known quality, such as contrast ratios, reflectivity and edge quality. Edge quality was of particular importance in development of the MTF curves for the mission. Among other things, the team would compare camera and satellite performance results to preflight measurements to determine if the equipment performed to expectations.

Mission reports

Upon completion of mission analysis, a final report was written by our people, detailing overall performance. These reports were written in several sections describing the PET team composition, mission goals, results and recommendations for the future. PET report formats were essentially the same for all missions, although their quality improved over time, as the team gained experience with data collection and analysis. Our people would also do quick scans of the imagery for target analysis and would clue the CIA team leader in, if they found something unexpected. Critical information was immediately transmitted to CIA headquarters, prior to publishing the final report or distribution of duplicate positive imagery.

It is recalled that 13 copies of each final report were printed. Among other destinations, two went to the CIA, one to NPIC, one to the camera contractor, one to Satellite Operations in Sunnyvale, CA, at least one to SAMSO and one was kept at AFSPPF. It is not recalled who got the remaining copies, but it is assumed that the NRO got their share, as well. Once again, these reports were ultimately used to establish contractor performance, assist in intelligence evaluation and improve or correct camera and satellite performance for subsequent missions.

R&D Directorate

The R&D Directorate was charged with developing new and advanced equipment and techniques for the entire operation. They also acted as a clearinghouse and honest broker for new ideas proposed by the intelligence community and their contractors, related to the processing and evaluation of photographic information. Of major concern was extracting the maximum amount of information from the developed film. Photographic film, used in all satellite missions, had the ability to hold over a thousand times more information than the human eye could see (a combination of resolution and gray scale).

Dual Gamma Processing

One major accomplishment of our facility was development of the concept of dual gamma processing. We called it Humpback Processing, at that time. This technique was developed to pull the maximum amount of information out of the original negatives and put it in the duplicate positives, in order to give the photo interpreters the best product to analyze. The concept was to pull the low exposure data up (higher gamma) to a visible level and pull the over exposed information back down (lower gamma) to a visible level and still maintain the resolution and grey scale needed to maintain an image suitable for photo interpretation and analysis. R&D engaged in an in-house, extensive research and testing effort to prove the concept, using actual imagery from Gambit missions (primarily CORN targets). We focused more on the low gamma process, since the high gamma part of the processing curve wasn't all that difficult to accomplish. Once the concept was established, it became a production-processing problem, which the QC Division solved. The result was a single processing curve (dual gamma) that eventually became the standard for duplicate positive film processing in the lab.

As we look back, through the now declassified literature and documentation, it appears that several other organizations adopted recognition of the concept and some may have claimed responsibility for its development. It seems that once a good idea leaks out, a whole lot of people are ready to jump in and claim credit for it. The facts are, however, we developed the basic ideas, ran an extensive test program to prove it out and presented it to higher-level officials. I know this, since I was the one who personally ran the test program and demonstrated the concept at AFSPPF. Of course, it's quite possible that other organizations were also working on the concept, independently of AFSPPF. Due to the security situation surrounding this whole operation, there is no way to know if this was the case. We were not advised of anyone else working on the original concept. All we can talk about is what we did and what we accomplished. Once the results of our work were presented to the CIA, it was out of our hands, other than continued refinement of data and rational in support of the concept.

Once the ball got rolling, many people and other organizations got into the act and, ultimately, the dual gamma concept was implemented. The NPIC had a comparison analysis study done on wet chemical vs. viscous dual gamma processing methods, for duplicate imagery, and couldn't tell the difference. Once use of the concept was authorized, our QC Division made it work in a production environment, using existing spray processing techniques and equipment. Since both approaches yielded the same result, our facility stayed with wet processing. This saved the government a considerable amount of money (multi millions) by not needing an entirely new viscous approach, proposed by Eastman Kodak. The dual gamma process was then implemented for use on Corona, Gambit and Hexagon duplicate imagery, for many years. The concept also worked on Original Negative imagery, as well, and it is believed it was implemented, accordingly. It is known that Kodak used a viscous approach to implement the process in their Bridgehead operation.

While R&D and QC personnel spearheaded the dual gamma concept and put it into operation, it should be noted that the entire facility participated in its success and can rightly take credit for it. The lab people processed the test film, as requested, and ran the H&D curves, the evaluation people performed the edge analysis required and management supported our efforts without interference. The entire project was run during off mission hours with the full cooperation of everyone involved. All those who worked on the project can be proud of the accomplishment, even though some probably had no idea what the objective was. They simply did what was requested, to the best of their ability, and that made it all work.

A famous line in a movie was "Build it and they will come". In our case, it was "Develop a good idea and it will be taken". Well, why not! After all, it was our job to develop good ideas and solve problems and we should be proud that they were taken and used. It is far better than having them taken and buried forever. Ok, so maybe I got carried away a little with the philosophizing, but you get what I mean. Congratulations to the entire team.

Microdensitometer

Early in the existence of AFSPPL, R&D personnel designed and developed the Microdensitometer. They contracted with the Data Corporation, Dayton, Ohio to production engineer it. This device was used to scan edges in the photography. The data was then used to provide a measure of the image quality. An IBM 360 computer was used to calculate the results. Data Corporation personnel, located within the facility, were instrumental in programming the computer to accomplish this task. The sharpness of the edges was a good measure of the mission's resolution and quality. This instrument eventually became an invaluable tool to measure mission quality, throughout the entire existence of the facility.

Computer Monitoring

The R&D Directorate designed and programmed a computerized monitoring system that was eventually installed in the photo lab to control and streamline the effectiveness of the operation. An IBM Model 1130 data-monitoring computer was purchased to accomplish this task. The cost of this system was around $150,000. You guessed it; computers were not cheap back in those days. R&D officers wrote all the software needed to monitor the lab functions, developed an error analysis routine to locate problem areas and designed various status reports for the many supervision levels within the facility. This system, primitive by today's standards, resulted in a huge savings in film resources, improved the quality of the product and provided lab and executive management with updated status reports of the overall mission.

Interestingly, today's cell phones have over a million times more computing power that that system ever had, yet it was efficiently programmed to do a remarkable job. R&D personnel had everyone in the facility tested for computer aptitude, in order to select a special crew to run the system during official missions. Upon selection, qualified lab NCOs took over the job of running this monitoring system. Key to its success was getting the NCOs onboard, which we did.

It must be noted, however, that when we used this system for the very first time, it crashed. This occurred around midnight or so on the first day. R&D personnel, including myself, were there when it happened and a bit of panic set in. Fortunately, we recorded values on the IBM punch cards before we ran them through the scanners, so we were able to reconstruct all the data, once the system was rebooted. The problem was it took until about 4 AM to get it done. Those of us involved got no sleep that night, and when the commander wanted to know what the heck happened with the $150,000 computer that was supposed to be so great and wonderful, we told him it was all part of the plan. He didn't expect this response and sort of just looked at us in disbelief. We explained that we purposely tried to crash the program to see what the vulnerabilities were, so we could protect against them in the future. We further mentioned that the system was still in the R&D phase and, since this was the first actual mission that we used it on, we expected problems. After all, nothing works perfectly the first time. When we told him we were reconstructing everything, from the data written on the cards following each roll of film, he started to buy the story. Seeing the info written on the cards helped to convince him. It took several more hours to get things running the way we wanted, with everyone using the cards properly, etc. Ultimately, it all worked and we got good results. Truth is, we were screwing around with the keyboard on the CPU, but had no idea it would cause such a catastrophic result. I think we invented the term "Computer Glitch" during this mission. The response to the commander was spontaneous on my part, but sometimes you just have to do that. There was some truth in there somewhere. All's well that ends well, however. By the way, writing all that data on the cards, as a backup, was a brilliant decision, I think.

Honest Broker

There were several development projects proposed by civilian contractors that had to be analyzed for need and reasonable chance for success. I cannot remember them all, but one does stand out that demonstrates the honest broker aspect of our mission. As I look back now, I still can't believe they even proposed such a device. Without going into boring detail, the essence of it was simply a special film spot scanning device that could scan imagery at speeds beyond the speed of light. Now that sounds like a great idea and would have solved a lot of problems. It would have been a very big help to our analysis mission. However, the most junior of physicists or physics students would have known that transmitting information faster than the speed of light isn't possible, at least not on this planet. They must have thought they were talking to administrators with no scientific abilities at all, or were just dumb enough to believe it themselves. When asked how they were going to achieve this feat, it was stated they were going to use a "Catadioptric" optical system that made it all work. This guy was a physicist and had a PH.D.? It didn't take very long to simply show him how wrong he was. Upon our rebuttal to his argument, in detail, including a reminder that such a system simply just used lenses and mirrors and was no big deal (it just sounded cool), he gave up and agreed we were correct. The project never got funded. I'm sure he was very embarrassed by it all, but he sort of had it coming.

As I look back, I often wonder how many similar projects get funded even today, because no one is there to technically evaluate them. Watch out for the next perpetual motion machine idea, now that the internet is in our lives. This is just one example. Eventually the word got around that "snow jobs" were in the past and the quality of proposed projects improved significantly. Oh yes, by the way, we never saw this guy again.

Exotic Projects

R&D also supported many aspects of the Corona, Gambit, Hexagon and other satellite programs to constantly improve their effectiveness. Many coordination meetings between the Air Force, CIA, Navy and other DOD organizations were hosted by R&D personnel in the facility. The many projects included new film processing techniques (such as Heat Processed Dry Silver), Free Radical film, high speed film scanning, Laser printing, Microwave drying, silver recovery from film, etc.

An exotic, advanced technique for color imaging on black and white film was also developed in the 1966 to 1967 time frame. This triple diffraction grating technique was very effective, but never actually implemented in satellite reconnaissance. The basic concept was to have imagery pass through three individual high resolution colored diffraction gratings (in each of the three primary colors), 120 degrees apart, and prior to being focused onto the film. The colors would essentially be encoded into the three gratings. Once processed as standard black and white imagery, the product would look just like standard black and white imagery. The grating lines would not even be visible, since their resolution would be much higher than the imagery, itself. Color would be achieved by passing a collimated beam of white light through the film, sending it through a lens and re-entering color back into the imagery by placing the appropriate color filters in the path of the three lines of spots at the focal point of the lens (Transform plane).

Yes, there is a lot more to the story and not all the technical details are described herein, but this gives one the basic idea. This technique made it possible to display false color or just select a single color. For example, if one were looking specifically for a red object, all other colors could be eliminated and the red object would pop up from the image. This could have been a big help to photo interpreters, in certain situations. Viewing could only be done on a light table or with a projector, which would have been no problem, since that was the dominant way of viewing reconnaissance imagery anyway. The concept was proven and effectively demonstrated, but apparently deemed to not be cost effective, since the demand was not there on a large scale. It is suspected, however, that this technique was developed and used by other small special project groups within the intelligence community.

The use and processing of color film was again looked into in 1969 by the '69 color committee (AFSPPF and CIA people served on this committee). There isn't too much to say about it now, except that it was a very slow, deep tank process only. Resolution of color film was nowhere as good as the standard black and white film (primarily due to the triple emulsion layer being a bit too thick). Imagery focused on the top layer would get a bit blurred by the time it got to the bottom layer. Black and white film has only one layer, which eliminates this problem. This problem isn't something one typically sees on commercial color prints, for personal use, however, since the resolution is far inferior to that possible with reconnaissance grade film. A color CORN target was also built to help evaluate the process.

Bottom line is, there was very little demand for the product and it never went into production. Black and white imagery remained the dominate medium for satellite reconnaissance. Had the photo interpreters really wanted color imagery, my opinion is the triple diffraction method, mentioned above, would have been the better choice, since it had much greater resolution potential, as well as providing a false color viewing capability. The technical details of either film or camera modifications could have been worked out.

Laser printing and Microwave drying

Laser printing was experimented with in the hopes of providing a sharper image and speeding up the process. A Niagara printer was modified with an Argon Laser as the primary light source. It turns out, however, that using a coherent, monochromatic light source had its problems. Our contact printing technique had its limitations. Contact between the O/N and the duplicate positive was only so tight. The Newton Ring problem (amplified by the use of a laser) was a bit too much to overcome and it was decided it wasn't worth the effort to continue the idea. The broader spectrum of non-coherent light, from a standard light source, worked much better.

Microwave drying had its problems, as well. It turns out that it was almost impossible to eliminate small droplets of water on the film during the drying process and, although this caused no problems with normal hot air blow-drying, it caused a big problem with microwave drying. These very small droplets of water would tend to boil, prior to evaporating and caused melted or burn spots in the film emulsion. There was no easy way to squeegee the water well enough to eliminate the problem. Although this effect is great for microwave ovens, for our everyday use, it was death for film drying. I must say, however, it was fun to play with these ideas.

An advanced look at high power lasers

I remember a visit to Raytheon Labs, in Waltham, MA, regarding the microwave drying idea. They were also working on a very powerful (I believe on the order of 10,000-watts or so) continuous beam, Infrared Laser and I got to see a demonstration of its effect. It could melt right through a firebrick in short order (Yes, I still have a souvenir brick showing it, but don't ask how I got it). It actually turned firebrick into glass. Check out the photos below. This is the actual brick used as a target for that LASER. Too bad, it broke in two, after all these years.

 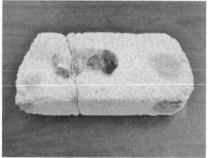

Short LASER bursts   LASER almost burned clean through
(Photo by Lloyd R. Spanberger)   (Photo by Lloyd R. Spanberger)

The scariest part of the demonstration was being in the room with it, as it was fired. It pretty much filled up the room, zigzagging back and forth through optical amplifiers, and I could just imagine what would have happened if one got a hand in the way of that beam (of course, extreme precautions were made). Laser weapons were under development at this time and this was proof positive, to me, that they were going to work. Notice the laser did not burn all the way through the brick, as you can see. Wonder why! What do you think would have happened, if the beam were allowed to burn completely through? Yea, you got it; it would just keep going and burn right through the building and beyond, including anyone who got in the way. Not a great plan, even back then. Now, they could have provided a back up brick, just in case, but I didn't see one there at the time. Who knows, maybe there was one in the next room or somewhere. Remember, these were the early days of development and scientists were not always that safety conscious as they are, I hope, today. Ok, maybe I got a bit too dramatic here.

Actually a few unlucky scientists were blinded by lasers in the very early days. I remember reading about it in an Electronic News publication, just after my boss and I both took a laser shot right between the eyes, on purpose, from about 100 feet away. This happened prior to my entering the Air Force, when I worked in a research lab after graduation from college. I know, what were we thinking? It was a Ruby Laser, I had built from scratch, and it just barely worked. Fortunately, it was only a short pulse and the beam was not that well focused. Once we read the article, we never did that again and bought special glasses to wear the next time we fired it. I must say, though, it was quite an exciting experience. Common sense showed up later in my career.

Astronaut Training

R&D personnel contributed, significantly, to the development of astronaut training techniques and systems, in conjunction with the NRO Dorian program. Once again, a few basic laws of physics were under attack and alternate approaches had to be taken. The training simulator project was on a path to nowhere. This was pointed out in a very large meeting of high-level people by yours truly, without a lot of political correctness. Well, it happens! I arranged a trip to Beale AFB in October of 1967, to show them a much more workable approach, similar to that used for the SR-71 training simulator. It was exciting and fun to actually sit in the SR-71 simulator and see what the pilots had to go through during their missions. It was the next best thing to actually flying in an SR-71. Shortly thereafter, however, the Dorian program, and the concept of a manned orbiting system for reconnaissance, was cancelled and replaced with the Hexagon satellite system. Based on a lot of factors, including the training problem, this was probably the best result for the program.

CORN Management

The R&D Directorate also managed the CORN network and directed the placement of portable targets around the country. The Data

Corporation, located in Dayton, Ohio, was the prime contractor supporting this program. As one can imagine, the timing and placement of these targets was extremely critical. The officer in charge of this program would get a call from the mission planners (believed to be SP-10, in Sunnyvale, California) and the fun began.

Lab R&D

The Lab, itself, engaged in a bit of R&D now and then, as well. Lab personnel developed modifications to the Dalton processors to increase the throughput speed from 40 ft/min to 100 ft/min. They also increased the film handling capacity of the Niagara printers from 500 to 1000 ft rolls. This may seem like a minor achievement now, but it was a big deal back then, when production speed was critical. Our facility then funded Kodak to incorporate the modifications in all machines. I bet you will never guess who never got credit for this, as well.

R&D Contracting

Most R&D efforts were conducted through contracted activity with the private sector. High priorities were placed on a speedy contract award process and in promoting competition to obtain the optimal design approaches and best prices. Traditionally, the Defense Department's contracting process consisted of the preparation of a statement of work, preparation of a procurement request, release of a request for proposals, conduct a source selection process (following the receipt of all contactor technical and price proposals), negotiations and, finally, contract award. This was a very time consuming process and was not acceptable for meeting the urgent demands of the AFSPPF for improved equipment and techniques for rapidly processing and fully exploiting our imagery.

Our approach, therefore, was to encourage carefully selected corporations from the private sector to consider submitting unsolicited proposals, which could be used for a contract award on a sole source basis. We, basically, prescreened our contractors and decided, in advance, who could deliver the best results. For the most part, many of them had no idea they were in competition with others. This approach greatly accelerated the contract award process and resulted in the early introduction of many technological advances in photographic printing, processing, and evaluation. This approach also eliminated the normal advertising requirements, which limited the exposure of our requirements to fewer contractors. This, in turn, helped us maintain security, as well as not having to work with less capable corporations who simply knew how to low bid a job. Although cost was a factor, high quality results were more important. By working with contractors in advance, the odds of success were significantly improved and costs were kept to a minimum.

Because of security restrictions, the AFSPPF R&D organization disguised its identity by processing many contract awards through the Reconnaissance Warfare (RW) organization of the Aeronautical Systems Division (ASD), at Wright Patterson AFB. Over time, many contracts were also awarded though the Photographic Laboratory organization also located at Wright Patterson AFB. An added benefit of this approach was that AFSPPF was able to obtain procurement, dispute resolution and the photoreconnaissance expertise of their personnel, at no additional cost. The contracting and negotiation expertise provided by Wright Patterson contracting officers was extremely helpful in expediting contract awards. As a result, our facility was very successful at holding down costs and managing our budgets, while developing state of the art equipment and techniques that met or exceeded mission requirements.

It should be noted that this contracting approach was not unique within the NRO/CIA Top Secret world of satellite reconnaissance. When time was of the essence and the mission was critical, these measures were necessary. To our credit, our organization was particularly good at it.

Logistics Directorate

The Logistics Directorate had responsibility for maintenance and supply. Their job may not have been very glamorous, but they were a key and necessary part of the organization and kept things running smoothly. The fact that there were few, if any, problems during the running of a mission, attests to their competency, as well as to the other divisions within the facility. Often, in most any organization, one doesn't get recognition unless a crisis occurs that they are responsible for solving. If no crisis pops up, it may appear that no one is doing anything, when the exact opposite is true. In our organization, we kept problems from occurring. It seems like all that did, other than provide outstanding service to the intelligence community, was keep us all the more invisible. One maintenance crisis did occur, however, that never made the news and it's possible the Commander never even knew about it. That story is related, as follows:

Thinking outside the box

The following story was written by former SSgt Lee Colville who worked in the Maintenance Division of our facility from 1960 to 1967. It's told in his own words.

"As many of you know, in today's world, many managers encourage their people to think "outside the box", in order to solve complex problems. Believe it or not, this concept was alive and well back in our days, as well. As most of you are now aware, AFSPPF was a tenant unit on Westover AFB and those of us working in it were unable to talk to a lot of people about our unique mission. We often had to solve their own problems quickly and quietly by being inventive and creative, and being able to "think outside the box". One such situation involved one of our processing machines (An Eastman Kodak HTA-3). Now, these machines were expensive and you don't just go to the corner store to buy a new one. Other machines of this type were working fine, but this particular one seemed to always produce scratches or chip spots on the film. We were in the beginning of a particular ORI (Operational Readiness Inspection) production mission, when the problem surfaced, and a bit of panic developed.

A multitude of people quickly got into the act and, after much discussion, those in the Photo Lab concluded that one, or several, of the machine's stainless steel rollers were causing the problem. We needed a short-term solution to get us through the mission and then we could work on a permanent solution, in a more relaxed atmosphere. After sufficient discussion and the weeding out of several dumb ideas, it was decided that the roller in question should be covered with something soft, in the hopes it would increase friction to stop the scratching (apparently the film was sliding over one of the rollers, somewhere in the machine, thereby causing the scratching). No one could figure out which roller it was, so it was decided to cover them all and get on with it. Of course, no one knew what to cover the rollers with, until the next dumb idea came up. After much colorful conversation and a bit of serious laughter (I suspect it had to do with some combinatorial use of the words "get on with it"), a young Airman, namely me, was sent to the base Commissary to buy a "box of condoms" (actually a Gross). To make this part of the story short, when the condoms arrived back in our unit, they were quickly put on all the rollers (yes, there was a lot more laughter taking place during this whole procedure, especially as to how it would be done and who was to do it). Ultimately, this solved the problem and the mission was completed without further incident. Of course, the used condoms were eventually discarded and you can imagine the dialog that ensued during that process. Love those dumb ideas. This situation soon led to the use of polyurethane rollers in the machine, which became a permanent fix. We never figured out which roller was the culprit, but no one cared any longer. No stainless steel ever touched the film again.

The truly unique part of the story, however, is the human-interest side. It turns out, that when I got to the on base Commissary, the female clerk, who I dealt with while ordering the condoms, was a family friend and the wife of a co-worker, former MSgt Gordon (Gordie) Pritchard. She was amazed that I wanted such an item and in such a large quantity. Unable to tell her why I needed them; my reply was just like so many others in dealing with people outside of the unit: "please, just get them and don't ask any questions". The most embarrassing part of this conversation was her laughter when I also said I wanted the largest condoms she had in stock. It was only after she picked herself up off the floor that I was able to get my purchase, attempt to get the redness off my face and get back to the unit, in time to fix the problem. I can only imagine what she had to be thinking all these years, not to mention the pillow talk that occurred that night. Oh yes, the joys of Top Secret work."

Civil Engineering Directorate

The following information was provided by former TSgt Robert (Bob) Sisson, who worked in the Utilities Division of this directorate from 1972 to 1976.

The four divisions within this directorate worked together to keep the infrastructure of the facility running smoothly at all times. They assisted each other regardless of their job specialties. There were carpenters helping plumbers, plumbers helping electricians, etc... There were times when the lead electrician would end up working on circuits while they were still hot, especially during active missions when equipment couldn't be shut down.

Electricians had to run power to new equipment and plumbers had to install chemical transmission lines using PVC, plastic, copper or stainless steel piping, depending on the chemicals involved. Sheet metal technicians had to construct lab tables and anything else needed. A lot of stainless steel was used throughout the facility. "I handled the Carpentry, along with two of my subordinates, and was the only locksmith in the organization. I worked on setting and changing combinations for vault doors, filing cabinets, fireproof safes, push button type cipher locks, etc."

Commander's conference room

"One project in 1973 was renovation of the commander's conference room to ensure that no sensitive information would leak outside the room during briefings. Col. Davison, our Commander at that time, did not have a secure conference room available in which he could talk about sensitive information. We took the conference room he had and totally revamped it by removing everything down to the block walls, concrete floor and ceiling. We put in a new sprinkler system and security baffles in all the heating and cooling ducts so sound would not travel through the ducts. We installed acoustic tiles on the walls and ceiling to absorb sound. We built and put up new chart frames on the walls that could be hidden behind sliding doors so he could step through a series of charts. We put in new Audio Video equipment and built new closets in the back of the room for their storage. When we were done, he had a perfectly secure conference room."

Chemical treatment

"In the latter years, we built a chemical treatment facility outside our building where our chemicals were transferred and treated. Civilian contractors built the basic facility for us. Afterwards, we had to go in and modify it to accommodate our special needs. We had two steam treatment vats that sat on stainless steel legs that were used for treating the chemicals we used during our missions. The two tanks came with roughly 100 or so polyurethane paddles, which would not hold up to the cooking process the chemicals had to withstand. I was approached one day and asked if I could make some paddles out of wood. Of course, I said yes. I tried to get some Cypress wood, which I soon found out was unavailable in Massachusetts. Plan 'B' was to use Birch. It took a while to get it done, but the new Birch paddles worked and exceeded our expectations."

Mulcher/Incinerator

"A specially designed mulcher/incinerator unit was used after each mission to destroy unwanted classified material. The Environmental Protection Agency got involved around 1974 and we had to install another burner in the incinerator section. Ultimately, there were three burning stages in the incinerator. The first stage ran at around 900 degrees F. The second stage ran around 1200 degrees F. The third stage ran at around 1800 degrees F. We operated and maintained this unit along with a very sophisticated fire warning and ionization detector system. We were the ones who would go into the pit after each mission and clean around the base of the mulcher section, remove all the stray film pieces, clean the area and make sure everything went into the Incinerator. There were always three personnel present for this procedure. Two went into the pit and one stood up top by the trap door, where a ladder dropped down into the pit. You guessed it, this hazardous and dirty work wasn't the most fun part of the job."

Escort Duty

"Our department was occasionally required to pull escort duty for outside contractors that entered the facility to do new construction or make repairs to existing utilities. If there was more than one individual working on a project, we had an escort with each individual while they were anywhere within the secure areas of the facility. Most of the time these locations were in the attic above the labs and other secure areas."

Extra Special Project

"Colonel Davison sent word to our shop one day that he wanted a plaque made for one of his deputies who was retiring and I wound up with the project. It turns out; our facility had a special color printer that could transfer a high quality image onto an aluminum film plate. We had a picture of the front page of the New York Times depicting the day that our astronauts first landed on the Moon. We used the picture of the front page of the New York Times dated Monday, July 21, 1969, as the image for the plaque. It wasn't too long after that when I was asked to make a 2nd plaque for another of our senior officers who was also leaving the organization. All total, there are now 12 such plaques in existence."

Vice Commander

The Vice Commander seemed to be involved in a variety of activities, but was primarily responsible for the sections as shown in the organizational chart. The Technical Director and Shipping reported up through the Vice Commander. See Chapters 9 and 5 respectively.

Special Activities

Special Activities were responsible for secure communications, and the scheduling of shipping and courier duty. In general, they were the operations group that coordinated the incoming and outgoing product and kept everything moving. Shipping, in turn, arranged for and scheduled all the courier planes for product delivery. A complete Top Secret communications center was maintained and operated in the facility to provide AFSPPF with covert communications within the NRO/CIA community. This system was totally independent and separate from normal Air Force Top Secret communications channels.

The entire AFSPPF worked in close coordination to accomplish their mission. It was a close-knit group of highly qualified and dedicated people. The senior NCOs required very little supervision and pretty much ran the photo-processing lab on their own.

Individual effectiveness reports were usually very general in nature. No detail of what anyone really did was included, due to the classified nature of the job. As a result, it was sometimes difficult for someone to get recognized for promotion or assignment to other jobs within the Air Force. Special re-assignments often had to be arranged outside of the normal system via word of mouth and personal connections. That's just the way it was.

Secure Communications (1814ᵗʰ Support Squadron)

The following information comes from the recollections of former MSgt Henry Leighow who served in our facility with a detachment of the 1814ᵗʰ Support Squadron from 1971 – 1976.

The 1814ᵗʰ Support Squadron was located on the 4ᵗʰ floor of the outer ring of the Pentagon, during this time. It assigned a detachment to AFSPPF, in the summer of 1968, to set up and maintain a separate and secure communication capability. This detachment continued to operate (Behind the scene) until the closing of the facility. There were approximately five to seven people assigned to this group and it was manned on a 24/7 basis. Their mission was to provide secure, top secret and unclassified communications between the facility and all of its various connections throughout the military, NRO, CIA and contractor organizations. A hotline was setup in the commander's office to allow instant communication to any of these organizations at any time. They were further tasked to begin providing support personnel to the Perkin Elmer Corporation, Danbury, CT, in support of the Hexagon program. This started sometime in the 1974 time frame.

From 1968 to 1970, they only had teletype (hard copy) communications. They were collocated in the Security office in 1970. This was in a separate vaulted room in the back of the facility. Here they set up and maintained a secure communications link between themselves, the Commander's office and Security, as well as to the outside world. Due to the facilities increasing support requirements to the NRO, equipment was upgraded by the addition of two Sperry Rand Univac 9300 computers with the capability to send and receive encrypted hard copy messages, 5" and 6" data reels and index cards. Secure transmission units were now tasked to operate on a 24/7 basis.

The unclassified teletype was used to primarily support the CORN program. Messages had to be sent out to contractors to advise them as to target locations and placement times, on a moment's notice. Secure communications of this nature were not always suitable, as the use of public phones was often needed. These calls never identified the caller or recipient. If one were to be listening in, they would have no idea what was going on, but the message got through. On one particular CORN target deployment, somewhere in the Southwestern desert area, the CORN targets were to be gathered up after dark, for whatever reason. As our contractors were doing their job, the local police discovered their presence and arrested them. The charge was (believe it or not) attempting to communicate with UFO's. One can only guess what they were thinking when they saw those big CORN targets spread out. Of course, they had no idea about our satellites. When the Communications guys got the eventual phone call, our security team solved the problem. They always seemed to do that and we never knew how they did it. I'm sure the local police are still scratching their heads about those targets.

Secure messages were primarily used for messages detailing the Satellite Film Bucket snatching and delivery schedules to Kodak, Perkin Elmer or our facility. Other messages dealt with duplicate negative delivery to our facility, mission scheduling, scheduling of meetings with NRO and CIA personnel, special secure travel scheduling, courier scheduling, etc.

Although largely unseen and kept locked up behind cipher locked doors, this support detachment provided a critical service to our facility and kept things running smoothly. When the facility was disbanded at the end of 1976, this detachment continued to provide support to the Perkin Elmer Corporation.

CHAPTER 5

"Ship It"

As mentioned earlier, The Special Activities section had the responsibility of scheduling the shipment of product to the designated customers. The Shipping department prepared the product for delivery and arranged the courier service to get it there. Their people often served as couriers, as well. There could be no mistakes in this operation. The right product had to get to the right customer as soon as possible. Organizationally, they came under the Vice Commander and primarily took their orders from Special Activities and possibly Operations.

Former Air Force Captain, Allen Ostdiek (Dept. officer in charge), hereby relates the story of the unique mission of this department, in his own words.

A View from the other side of Production

"In the booklet "A Brief History" (The National Reconnaissance Office at 50 Years), a notation is made of CIA director, Allen Dulles, unrolling film from the first successful satellite photoreconnaissance mission, Corona 14, before president Dwight D. Eisenhower in the White House. It must have been a dramatic and proud display of the technology and physical accomplishments of U. S. capabilities of the time. The accomplishments and advancements of the camera systems, the rocket progression, the chemical understanding of photo emulsions were all outstanding and impressive for the time.

This is an abbreviated review of those accomplishments in the AFSPPF "Shipping" Dept. For all the work of the best and brightest would have been for naught if that work didn't get to the people who needed it. The men in the "Shipping" Dept. of AFSPPF handled the product of all the work done by the facility. This is a short review of their contribution to the mission.

The expertise of making duplicate copies for the Intelligence experts across the U. S. military and civilian field is well documented in this essay. The facility was told how many copies of specific target areas were needed and where to deliver these copies. However, little consideration was given to what happened to all that film as it exited the "Lab" and went to that area of AFSPPF known as "Shipping".

A simple conveyer system transferred the film from the processing lab to the Shipping area thru an underground tunnel below the main hallway of the facility. Once there, film canisters were simply arranged on cabinets, according to ID labels. Once the Mission was completed, the men would simply use the "Shopping List" to load boxes for specific customers, then seal boxes and identify customers who were to receive that box. Once organized, the system worked well. A major problem was that the system was sometimes threatened because of boredom.

Whereas the photo lab was staffed by men who were highly trained in the photo technology sciences, the men who did the actual packaging and delivery were primarily men assigned to AFSPPF because of their security clearance. Many were first term airmen returning from some remote assignment in Europe or Asia and having less than a year or so left, on a 4-year tour of duty. The young men doing the work were highly intelligent (many being foreign language experts). The work was not especially intellectually challenging and this 'mundane' work was met with an unwritten attitude I tried to instill that might be categorized as "Yes, almost anyone could do this job, but very few could do it time after time after time . . . correctly each time". Often, the Lab was under pressure to complete a Mission 'yesterday' because of whatever was on the film. When that happened, the Shipping Dept. was expected to deliver it 'day-before-yesterday'. Over the years, there was never a security leak due to a failure in the delivery system.

The vast majority of product was delivered via Air Force planes (Military Airlift Command at McGuire AFB) and a rather routine, consistent path was established over time with variations because of special needs at specific times. "Couriers", who were senior NCO's and Junior Officers, accompanied all product deliveries.

The "classified" communication link was also housed in the shipping area to take advantage of this secure area in the building. All classified 'news', 'orders', and 'information' of all types came into or left the Facility, via this route.

An effort to show the "human" face of the unit and to better understand some of the Shipping Division's story is given here in several short stories, in the hopes that some AFSPPF veterans may remember and identify with.

Supplies and Work Space

While the packing system of stacking cans of film on top of one another on a cabinet worked just fine, it certainly didn't look sophisticated at all. It was certainly not worthy of the millions of dollars spent on the total program. As such, the engineers came up with a system of racks whereas the cans of film could be separated, loaded from the back, flow forward to the front on an incline, and picked there for loading into boxes. Sounds simple enough, but the problem was in trying to describe to the contractor what we wanted without telling him what we do. "Why", was the most used word from the contractor, and "just because" was the most used response.

For some reason, the Shipping Division had the responsibility of getting the film ID labels ordered. It was an interesting situation figuring out how to identify the revolution of the satellite and the target location . . . without using any words to do so. A system, understood by both the Lab and Shipping was arrived at, and labels ordered.

Color Code

When Mission product was packaged, there were no addresses on any box. Each box had a colorful label on it. Each color indicated a different customer. Our aircraft personnel would frequently look at them and inquire who was going to get what. When the courier would say he "didn't know" (which often was true), they would, more often than not, go away shaking their heads.

Waste Disposal (Not an easy task)

Even the most efficient photo-processing lab in the world has a certain amount of 'waste' material inherent in the process. The problem of disposing of the classified (Top Secret) waste material was one not easily or usually appreciated. For years, AFSPPF reserved the base burn facility for a full day each week. Junior officers and airmen were detailed to burn all the classified material (99% film). The base's facility was not built to handle the volume of classified film we needed to destroy. This was film used to calibrate the processing machines and never meant for delivery to customers. Although the men used ingenious methods to reduce miles of film into ash on a regular basis, an occasional visit to the base hospital was required, to care for burns caused by molten plastic that used to be highly classified film. The 'burn pit' would be known to 'huff and puff' better than any fairytale wolf and as the smoke poured from the chimney, modern day environmentalists would have a heart attack, if they watched. Men would come back covered with black soot and would cough up black spit for days.

Chip It

The mere volume of film, to dispose of, called for a better method to handle it all. A 'one-of-a-kind' incinerator was designed to burn such classified material. The engineers soon learned that an off-the-shelf chipper could not handle a roll of 9.5-inch film as it could handle a tree branch. The system was designed in two parts: #1: a chipper to cut up the film and allow small pieces to drop into a holding bin, #2: the furnace. The off-the-shelf chipper purchased could handle tree trunks up to 18 inches in diameter. The 'teeth' were about 10 inches long, 2 inches wide and 3 inches deep powered by a very powerful motor that put a jet engine to shame, considering the noise level. However, when the first spool of 9.5-inch film was tossed in, the noise must have been heard miles away and we were lucky no one was killed by those teeth that were broken loose and being shot all around the room like bullets.

The chipper was immediately destroyed and everyone went back to the drawing boards. Ultimately, the chipper was made tough enough to handle the density of a roll of film and the system worked.

I can't recall the name of the office in the photo lab, but the young men there seemed grateful when we walked into their chemistry lab with a 'chunk' of material we pulled from the furnace, after a 'burn', to have it analyzed. Seems they enjoyed having a "real" chemical problem to solve. Ended up that chunk of material was "silver". We indeed, developed a classified film disposal and silver recovery system.

Again not a single security breach occurred in handling the miles of film marked for destruction. (A more complete, technical report of this project could have been included in this report, but from the view of laymen, this is our story, and we're sticking to it.)"

Supply . . . and the "R & D" Arm of Eastman Kodak

Now . . . The Rest of the Story

Note: It is not the intent to disparage Eastman Kodak (EK) with this inclusion, but it is written to prove once again, *"there are two sides to every story"*. As told to AFSPPF's Chief of Supply Officer, Blaine Thacker and others, during a trip to EK in Rochester, New York.

EK played a huge role in the U.S. Satellite Reconnaissance program and it may be fair to say the program would not have been as successful as it was, without their expertise. As well as running the Bridgehead facility, they manufactured the film AFSPPF used for its Missions. Typically, the film would be shipped to Westover AFB via bulk shipments, but at times, special priorities created an emergency requirement and AFSPPF personnel would end up driving to Rochester, NY to pick up what was needed. The following is what we learned during one of those trips:

Eastman Kodak and the civilian 'retail' market

The manufacturing of reconnaissance film was done in large sheets (i.e.: 10- 20 feet wide). It was then cut down into the required lengths and widths that the "military" needed. As with any manufacturing process, there were times when there were 'bad spots' (or manufacturing defects) in the large sheets of film emulsion. EK took the 'best' parts of a particular run and filled the orders for the military (AFSPPF) and then took whatever was left over (the scraps) and cut them down further into retail lengths and widths to sell to civilians for their personal cameras. It was understood that this process was how EK first got into the retail market. We have all purchased 35mm film from retail stores for our personal use, but none of us realized that was made possible because of the military contracts with AFSPPF. As large as it was, retail film sales were secondary as the primary purpose for manufacturing film was for the military.

Maintenance R&D

The following story was told by Capt. Blaine Thacker, and verified by Sgt. Leroy (Moose) Miller during one of the brainstorming sessions, at the 2012 AFSPPF reunion, in Branson, Missouri.

AFSPPF needed a large Maintenance Division, ostensibly to keep the film processors running in the lab. Made sense, and looked appropriate on the Air Force registers. It so happens, AFSPPF had personnel from

EK on its premises much of the time. Their job was to watch and learn what we were doing to "develop and build" one-of-a-kind film processors (Prototypes). It is believed that AFSPPF was the only place in the world that processed and developed these large rolls of film and, therefore, it had to create and build unique film processors to do the job, which was done on the premises of the facility. Sgt. Miller noted that it was interesting to see the "NEW" processors EK sold to AFSPPF, as they were periodically needed. It was observed that they were often reproductions of what innovations AFSPPF had already designed, maybe the year before. "And we paid plenty of money for them", he added. Thus said, tongue-in-cheek, looks like AFSPPF was an unofficial R&D arm of Eastman Kodak, as in reality, it was. Once again, our people did the work, but got no credit or pay for it.

Courier Duty

Yes, we all did it and the following are stories from the personal experiences and recollections of Allen Ostdiek and former Air Force Capt. Blaine Thacker, who worked in the Supply Division:

As mentioned earlier, the entire unit was involved with the duties of delivering Mission product. Junior Officers and Senior NCO's were detailed the responsibilities. The Unit never suffered a Security breach during its existence. Many of the trips were routine and maybe a little boring, but a few included some interesting moments.

Skiing Mt. Tom (Allen Ostdiek)

"It was cold, I think it was December and there was snow on the ground, as a C130 was making its way home from Rochester, New York after the sun set in the western sky. It was a beautiful evening and the flight crew was kind enough to let one of the couriers sit with the pilots and navigator to experience the flight. The lights of New York City were impressive from the sky and soon the plane closed-in on Westover, a person could hear the pilot talking to the Westover control tower.

PILOT: "No, I can't see the lights yet, must be a little further out than you thought".
TOWER: "I'll check, but the runway lights should be on, wait a second. OK, how about now"?
PILOT: "OK, I think I see them. Ya, there they are, but they don't seem real bright".

After a little time;

PILOT: "Those lights sure look a little wavy to me, kinda like a hill side".

All this time, the courier was also looking for the lights and when the pilot noted the lights looked like they were on a hill, something connected.

COURIER: (On the side, to the Navigator) "Um, just outside Westover, there is a ski area, called Mt. Tom and they light up their slopes at night for night skiing."

NAVIGATOR TO PILOT: "Sir, I understand there is a ski slope just outside Westover and they light the slope at night. Are we sure what we're looking at?"

PILOT: "OK, maybe I'll look around a little . . . 'Oh, over there a couple of degrees, nice straight lights, bright and beautiful . . . think we'll use them. Tower, we're coming in . . .'"

The Product was safely delivered once again and "the Unit That Didn't Exist" continued its task of supplying timely information to the U. S. Intelligence Community and all on board was unharmed. There was no point in trying to land on a ski slope anyway, since the plane didn't have any skis."

Who's In Charge Here? (Allen Ostdiek)

"AFSPPF received a high degree of importance in the overall military chain of command because of its mission. It was evident in many ways, but that 'importance' became very clear one bright, crisp Autumn Saturday morning, when a C130 aircraft landed at Westover and was met with men, from the Shipping Dept., and Couriers, with only enough product to fill the back of a pickup truck. When the pilot of the plane came around to see his cargo, he became incensed at the puny load for his trip. It turns out; this was an unusually small load. We normally shipped multiple pallets of material requiring a large aircraft. Actually, we would simply tell MAC (Material Air Command) what we had, in approximate size and weight, and they assigned planes to handle the job. He demanded to know why we requested such a large plane for such a small amount of cargo and we were not going any place until he found out why. While he was contacting his headquarters, I inquired as to the reason for his unhappiness and found out that he and his crew was scheduled for a two-week tour of duty in Hawaii, before our call came for service. Their orders were changed from a nice two week trip to Hawaii to a day or so of running around the U.S., making take-offs and landings. When he returned, we were told to finish loading and he took off without another word. We have no idea what transpired between him and his boss, but the problem was suddenly solved."

Bubble Gum (Blaine Thacker)

"We were assigned aircraft from both the Air Force and Navy, to minimize attention to our travels. Often, the "Load Masters" (NCO's assigned to those aircraft) were trying to find out "what we had in the boxes" that we were transporting and dropping off, at multiple locations throughout the USA. My answer was always "Bubble Gum" (which would send the NCO's into orbit) . . . I actually had to "pull my gun" out of my flight suit one time in order to keep the Load Master from "opening" one of our boxes. The aircraft commander (pilot) about lost it when he came down into the cargo area and saw what was going on. I mean, what else would you do if someone were trying to mess with your Top Secret "Bubble Gum"? The pilot and crew quickly got the message and the mission proceeded without further incident."

Interservice Co-operation (Blaine Thacker)

"On one delivery mission, the plane was from the Navy and the "flight crew" decided that they would not take me back to Westover AFB after we had made all of our drops, because the crew was a NAVY crew out of Virginia somewhere. I had to get on the radio from the cockpit and call a General officer (cannot remember his name). The general got on the horn with the Aircraft commander (a Lt Col) and told him in so many nice words: "TAKE THAT COURIER BACK TO WESTOVER". After landing at Westover, the pilot did not shut down their engines, he just had me step out the 'back loading ramp' as they kept moving and departed shortly thereafter. Thanks a lot! The Navy does its mission . . . but sometimes they needed to be told "exactly" what that mission was."

Eddie's Chop House (Allen Ostdiek)

"Volume wise, the vast majority of mission product was delivered via aircraft. However, approximately 50% of the actual courier trips were probably made via ground vehicles. In the beginning . . . most ground trips were made with the personal autos of the couriers (they were paid mileage, of course). With the passage of time, vehicles were rented (Avis, Hertz or a local rental agency) and, at times, civilian trucks were rented, as well. Most ground trips involved two days (one day driving each way with a pickup or delivery made at the beginning or end of each day).

One particular day, on the New York Thruway, we came upon a 'traffic jam' with no obvious reason that we could see. As we crept forward, eventually, we saw that the Highway Patrol was searching each vehicle and when our turn came, the official wanted to see what our cargo was in the truck. I declined to allow him visitation rights to the truck's interior and he did not appreciate my action. We were escorted to the side of the road and a discussion followed. I showed him my ID, and orders, and when he still insisted on 'seeing' the cargo, I asked him to call our security officer, Col. Tom Taylor (which I was told was one of our last lines of defense). I was not privy to the phone call, but after some time, the officer returned and we were allowed to continue our way home (Never did find out just what Col. Taylor said to him).

"Eddie's Chop House" was mentioned in the beginning of this story, because most (if not all) couriers visited that fine eating establishment at least once, at the end of a long day's drive. Having a fine meal and indulging in a nice libation was a great way to end the day.

Some courier trips were needed sort of on a "spur of the moment basis", with no time for planning. These often involved cargo of no more than an envelope or two. Most occurred without incident, but on one occasion a car broke down "deep in the heart of Connecticut", and in a neighborhood many would question before stopping. Remember, these are days before GPS and Cell Phones were even thought of. Well, a little walking to find a phone and a little coordination between AFSPPF and others, and all was well, but I think the incident led to the decision to 'rent' vehicles after that."

Dedication (Allen Ostdiek)

"The quality, efficiency and volume of work were well established for AFSPPF. They all affirm the dedication of all personnel that worked at the facility. However, one incident connected to the delivery service gives an additional indication of the type of people that gave dedicated service to their country while assigned to AFSPPF.

One senior NCO, just newly assigned to AFSPPF, was tapped for duty on a particular courier mission. He reported with his partner and completed the mission, without comment. The day after the plane returned, he was on sick call, but returned after that, doing his normal duties. Several months later, his name came up again and the same scenario happened, and happened again for a third time. By now, it was realized that this NCO (with over 25 years of Air Force experience) suffered severe "air-sickness" on each flight. When asked why he didn't report his sickness, he replied that he didn't want anyone to think he would 'shrink' from his duties and that sickness was a small price to pay for the completion of the mission. Now that's dedication for you."

Oklahoma? (Allen Ostdiek)

"To the best of my knowledge, Oklahoma has never been a hot spot in the Intelligence, or Reconnaissance world. Courier experience varied from routine trips to nights spent on disabled planes, as happened one night in Oklahoma. Most delivery trips were started early in the morning and with any luck at all, the plane would return before nightfall. However, one particular day we found out, before leaving the facility for the day, that the plane, along with my two couriers, would not be able to return that night . . . at all. The plane developed mechanical problems in the air and an Air Force base in Oklahoma was the nearest place to land.

I was sitting in my comfortable home enjoying the evening. It so happened that my wife and I were having a few friends over for supper. By the time our guests left, I must have had nearly a dozen phone calls concerning the unexpected stop and I was questioned, by my guests, if this was a normal job situation. The answer was a smile and shrug of the shoulders. What was I supposed to say or do, anyway?

I never found out the exact nature of the problem, but our two couriers spent the night on the plane and in the morning, a substitute aircraft picked them up and completed their deliveries. The couriers were very grateful for the local Air Force personnel, who made meals and blankets available to them, throughout their ordeal. It was nice to know we had friends in Oklahoma.

From now on, when someone informs you of their work in a "Shipping" department, please give them a little respect. It really isn't all that easy."

CHAPTER 6

A Day in the Life

One of our members, and major contributor to this history, Lt Col, USAF (Ret.), Alfred (Al) C. Crane, wrote what it was like during a typical day in the life of our members assigned to the facility. It goes like this:

A day in the life, during a typical mission:

"If you haven't worked in a "Clean Room" with full "Bunny Suits" in a toxic chemical environment for 13 hours a day, weeks on end, you can't appreciate what the men of AFSPPF experienced in a day in day out basis, during a typical mission.

The term 24/7 hadn't been invented yet, but those of us who worked in the DOD, CIA, and Military service photographic processing laboratories experienced that fact of life, at some level, during their career. Working out of tents, trailers, and fixed facilities processing "short rolls of "Tac Recce" film (50-250 ft), little jobbers (U-2 6,000 ft), and NRP satellites 20,000 ft of original negative imagery and multiple copies of duplicate positive/negative imagery and film products.

At Westover, we would come in for our shifts, clear through security, receive shift mission briefings, change into full "Bunny" Clean Room suits and proceed into the Laboratory. Processing, production control, and quality control personnel would work in the various rooms designated for film duplication, printing, processing, quality control, labeling, shipping and distribution. Each foot of film processed was evaluated by a qualified quality control technician/manager for defects and tonal quality before acceptance/rejection. Film that didn't meet established standards was rejected for later classified destruction and an order to reprint & process the subject film was issued.

A full complement of maintenance personnel were always ready to come into the lab, whenever, to fix problems on the spot. Their workshop was always busy working on new equipment and equipment that needed to be repaired and sent back to the production floor. Another full complement of technicians was on duty operating the Chemical Mixing (Chem Mix) area, constantly mixing, performing chemical analysis and transferring the processing chemicals to the production area. A full chemical analysis laboratory was manned during each mission to assist in the quality control process.

Statistics on film production (how many cans of film to each designated customer (up to 30)) and quality control were constantly monitored and posted for both production and management personnel to help manage the production of each mission (bucket of film).

The Shipping Section catalogued all processed film products and quality control personnel checked that each designated customer had the exact number of copies that they were assigned by the NRO and other military services. The film cans were then loaded on pallets to be sent via special courier aircraft from Westover AFB to designated distribution points.

Depending on the mission (Corona, Gambit or Hexagon), the facility would be in full production mode for weeks and, in some cases, a month at a time. In between missions, installation of new equipment, maintenance of existing equipment, and continuous training of personnel would occur.

The facility also supported the Performance Evaluation Teams (PET) and evaluation of new techniques, equipment, and processes from the R&D directorate in direct support of the NRO/CIA during "down times" and, in many cases, during mission production. The only time the facility was actually down was from Christmas Eve until the day after Christmas.

A favorite memory of mine, was reporting for my shift in the cold of winter, and after 14 hours in the lab, seeing the next shift in the change room wearing "Mukluks" and parkas covered in snow! Then, I had to dig out my car, under several feet of snow, before going home to get a few hours of rest before reporting for the next shift. Of course, being in the military, we had to keep all personnel and medical appointments prescribed and, in our "spare" time, have some "free time" with our families and friends.

We also performed courier duty accompanying production and R&D film products throughout the Continental United States (CONUS), as well as TDYs to other NRO & DOD units both in CONUS and overseas, to assist them in reconnaissance film production, and to write USAF photographic and image quality control regulations, procedures, and techniques.

We could never share our experiences and mission with family, friends, or fellow service members (unless properly cleared and with a need to know). We did have, however, a close relationship with our fellow facility members, in family events, picnics, sharing births & family experiences, ball teams, golf, fishing and rod & gun club activities, to name a few. I used to ride with several NCOs on our motorcycles (I had a Honda 350SL.). Of course, we participated in military functions, such as, Dining Outs, Picnics, Retirements, Promotions, Awards Ceremonies, etc.

We were all "GI's". We lived with low pay, long hours and no formal recognition, but we had PRIDE in our contributions to our Country and the Cold War. Many of us served in Vietnam, Thailand and other overseas locations before, during and after our tours at AFSPPF. Such was our life back then."

CHAPTER 7

Programs We Supported

SATELLITES

SAMOS

We were originally created to support the **SAMOS** Satellite program. SAMOS was not a film return satellite. It developed the film onboard the spacecraft, scanned it with an optical high-speed spot scanner and transmitted the information down to an earth receiving station, for rescanning onto photographic film, for interpretation and analysis. It was the first attempt to accomplish satellite reconnaissance without returning film directly. Ultimately, the technique proved to be of low quality and way ahead of its time. The technology wasn't up to speed to support the concept. Aside from low image quality, the download data rate wasn't fast enough to get sufficient data down to an earth station during the short time a satellite was in position from orbit. The image processing technique used here was an early version viscous approach, similar to that used in the old Polaroid cameras.

NASA, however, used this concept, via a separate relationship with the Eastman Kodak company, to photograph the lunar surface with five orbiting spacecraft, in the mid 1960's. The image quality from this technique, although insufficient for detailed earth reconnaissance, was good enough to allow NASA to photograph almost the entire surface of the moon and establish the landing spot for the first lunar landing. The data rate requirement was much lower for this type of mission, since a satellite orbiting the moon was in contact with an earth receiving station for a much longer period.

Somehow, the NRO apparently allowed Kodak to use the SAMOS imaging and readout technique for this unclassified NASA mission. Strange things do happen, for the good. The Moonscape photo shown, from a lunar recon mission, is from my personal files. Somehow, it just showed up at some point in my Air Force career and I tucked it away. Sometimes things just happen like that. I now wish I had tucked more things away, but back then, I doubt the writing of this history was on anyone's mind, let alone mine.

Composite Moonscape photo from a SAMOS type system
(NASA Photo)

CORONA

The Corona (KH-1-4) (KH denoted Keyhole, the name of the program's security system) satellite program was the original mainstay program for the facility, once it became operational. ITEK Corporation was the prime contractor for the Corona camera. The first dozen missions of the Corona program were total failures, except for the lessons learned. Failures had to be analyzed without the benefit of seeing the actual hardware that failed or could have caused the failure. After all, it was stuck in space or burned up upon re-entry. This posed quite a problem for the scientists and engineers back on earth. No doubt, there was a lot of conjecture back and forth between the people responsible for identifying and fixing the problems. One can only imagine the arguments and finger pointing that took place over twelve failed missions. The fact that the program survived is a small miracle. Can you picture all those bean counters arguing about all that wasted money, on this pipe dream, and how this program would never get off the ground (literally)?

Once Corona started to deliver product (Mission 14, KH-1) in mid August 1960, our facility went into full swing. Note that mission 13 was successful in all respects; however, there was no film onboard, for whatever reason. It demonstrated the first successful bucket recovery, however.

Corona was a CIA run system and was used for broad area search missions. It was launched into a polar or near polar orbit. Its total orbital time was typically measured in days, but was extended later in life due to incorporation of a dual bucket design (KH-4A). In the beginning, it also served in a detailed reconnaissance mode, since that's all there was. It used 70 mm wide film throughout its lifetime. Resolution, in today's standards, was not very good, but it did the job. Once Gambit came into operation, it took over the job of high-resolution imaging of key targets, for detailed analysis. Corona was then in a mode of strictly looking for change or anything new and Gambit was charged with getting details.

Note: The different Corona KH numbers simply denoted improvements in cameras and reentry vehicles, etc. The name Corona refers to the KH series 1-4. KH-5 was the Argon satellite and KH-6 was the Lanyard satellite, both of which are not discussed in this book, since they were not significant contributors to the overall reconnaissance program. Of course, that's just my opinion.

AFSPPF created duplicate positive imagery for Corona throughout its existence (1960 to 1972). Of special note, independent of Kodak's Bridgehead, AFSPPF processed the original negatives and created all the duplicate positives from the last three Corona missions, from Jan to May 1972. The program was declassified in 1995 by President Clinton. The Corona satellite is now on display in the Smithsonian Air and Space Museum in downtown, Washington DC. A Corona film return "Bucket" is on display in the Smithsonian National Air and Space Museum, Udvar-Hazy Center, near the Dulles Airport in Chantilly, VA.

QUILL

Quill was the world's first radar imaging satellite ever flown (For technical details, please see the related publications on the NRO web site). The program, itself, was established as a feasibility study to see if a synthetic aperture radar (SAR) could be used to do post bomb damage assessment, in an all weather environment. The satellite used technology from the Corona program. The radar-collected data was transferred to photographic film on board and the film bucket was then dropped back down to earth, as in the Corona program. Two missions were planned, but only one was needed, since the data collected on the first flight was so perfect. All technical objectives were met with a single mission and the system performed far better than program expectations.

The first and only mission was launched in mid December 1964. In a matter of a few days, 14 data collection passes were made, of which 7 were recorded on film. All data collection passes were over the CONUS, in the Northeastern and Western US. The film bucket was dropped near the end of December and the despooled film sent to AFSPPF for processing. It arrived on the morning of 24 December, Christmas Eve. Thanks a lot guys! The film was processed and then sent to a secure facility where a specially made precision optical processor was used to convert the recorded data to usable imagery. Once again, our facility quietly did its job without incident. The satellite was destroyed upon re-entering the atmosphere in mid January 1965.

GAMBIT

Gambit (KH-7-8) was an Air Force run system and used 9.5-inch film throughout its history (1963 to 1984). These satellites were launched into near polar orbits. Gambit 1 (KH-7) was a single bucket system, which could stay in orbit up to a week or more. It was eventually improved to the Gambit 3 (KH-8) model, which had a higher resolution capability, developed into a two-bucket system, and incorporated a terrain-mapping camera (using 5-inch film). Later in its life, mission duration went from less than a week to several months. In a pinch, it could be shot into a higher orbit to help serve as a search system. The two-bucket version doubled the orbital life. There were no other Gambit versions. It turns out Gambit 2 and 4 were optional proposals that never got implemented.

Eastman Kodak was the prime contractor for both Gambit cameras and Lockheed was the prime contractor for the satellite. Gambit was programmed to photograph targets specified by another special projects group in Sunnyvale, CA. It looked at specific strategic targets of interest to our intelligence experts. Some of these targets were being monitored on a routine basis to follow construction progress or track activity therein. Others were designated based on findings of the Corona and Hexagon imagery indicating something new and of potential strategic importance. In any case, Gambit took very high-resolution images of its targets, compared to the much lower resolution from the Corona search system. Ultimately, Gambit produced the highest resolution of all film return satellites over the entire length of their existence. AFSPPF created duplicate positive imagery for Gambit, from conception to the end of 1976, when the facility was shut down.

Gambit 1	Gambit 3
(Photo by Jessica L. Davis)	(Photo by Jessica L. Davis)

HEXAGON

Hexagon (KH-9) (1971 to 1984) was a CIA run satellite that went into operation during the time Gambit was flying and the two of them worked in conjunction with each other, to get the job done. Perkin Elmer was the prime contractor for the Hexagon camera, ITEK for the mapping camera and Lockheed was the prime contractor for the satellite. Management of the Hexagon program was transferred to the Air Force in late 1973. Hexagon used 6.6-inch film for the stereo panoramic cameras and the mapping camera, which was installed later in the program, used 9.5-inch film. It also had a stellar camera on board that used 70 MM film. The hexagon satellite was very large, about the size of a school bus. It was affectionately known as "Big Bird".

Hexagon was launched into a near polar, sun-synchronous orbit, which, basically, meant that the shadows of objects on the ground did not change over time. This was a big help to the photo analysts. Hexagon served the roll as a higher resolution search system as well as a detail collection system, with Gambit still providing extremely high-resolution images for detailed analysis. Hexagon contained four main film return buckets and later a separate bucket for the mapping camera film. It could stay in orbit for many months, vs. the limited life of Corona and Gambit.

The Hexagon satellite was also the first to test an early version of an electro-optical sensor, now commonly used in today's systems. A prototype device, using this sensor, was piggybacked on one of the later Hexagon missions. Data was transmitted back down to earth as it is in today's systems. There was no re-entry bucket and no film was involved. Perkin Elmer was the prime contractor for this device, which used an early version of CCD (charge-coupled device) technology, much like the digital cameras of today. The technology was in its infant stage at that time and had many problems to overcome, prior to becoming reliable in the space environment. Note that this technique was significantly different from that used by the SAMOS satellite, which also transmitted data down to earth. Electronics technology was improving, at this point, and download data rates were much higher, allowing this technique to become viable.

Note that commercial grade technology becoming available doesn't mean it can be immediately used in a military or space environment. Military grade electronic components require the ability to operate extremely reliably in a harsh, wide temperature range environment with limited variation of performance specifications. Space grade components have similar environmental operating requirements, along with the fact they must operate under high 'G' forces (during launch and reentry) and in zero gravity (on orbit). Loose miniscule particles cannot be allowed to float around inside the casing of components and potentially short out circuits. Remember, in a zero gravity environment, everything floats, even dirt. These components must be designed to counteract these problems and are not necessarily as available as their commercial counterparts are. This situation applies to entire electronic systems, as well as their components. Reliable operation in space is critical. One cannot or could not simply replace a bad component or system, as in a commercial system, especially back then. Repairmen just couldn't get there. The technology today is far superior and these problems are now minimized.

Gambit and Hexagon worked together throughout the lifetime of Hexagon (1971 to 1984). Both programs launched their last satellites in mid 1984. The final attempt to launch a Hexagon satellite was in April 1986, however, due to a booster failure, the entire mission was lost. This marked the end of the Film Return Satellite era.

Hexagon Qualification Model in the National Museum of the US Air Force
(Photo by Timothy M. O'Brien)

Declassification of the Gambit and Hexagon programs occurred on 02 June 2011 via a document signed by Bruce Carlson, director of the NRO, at that time. Both the Gambit and Hexagon satellites were loaned to the National Museum of the US Air Force, Wright Patterson Air Force Base, located in Dayton, Ohio. There was a commemorative program at the museum on 26 January 2012 whereby Bruce Carlson and other speakers from the NRO and industry described several aspects of the program. The author of this document, Lloyd Spanberger, a former Air Force Captain and research physicist, formerly assigned to the R&D Directorate of AFSPPF, spoke for just under ten minutes explaining the mission of our organization and our contribution to the National Reconnaissance Program (See figure below). Apparently the speech went over fairly well, as many people wanted to ask questions and talk about our organization for well over an hour, after the ceremony. The display in the museum consists of Gambit 1, Gambit 3 and the qualification model of the Hexagon Satellite, for all to see. It is scheduled to remain there indefinitely.

The following two photos represent somewhat of an introduction of the Gambit and Hexagon satellites in the National Museum of the US Air Force, located at Wright Patterson Air Force Base in Dayton Ohio. The third photo shows the author of this book presenting the story of our facility. They were taken during the commemorative presentations on 26 January 2012.

COLD WAR IN SPACE

TOP SECRET RECONNAISSANCE SATELLITES REVEALED

During the Cold War, the US relied on photo reconnaissance satellites to track adversaries' weapons development, especially in the Soviet Union and China. From the early 1960s to mid-1980s, photography from space was often the only way to get critical data about nuclear threats.

The National Reconnaissance Office, Department of Defense, US Air Force, Central Intelligence Agency, and industry worked together to create amazingly complex and capable satellites. Intelligence gained from these systems proved critical in winning the Cold War.

These satellites' powerful cameras used long rolls of thin plastic light-sensitive film to make photo negatives—the cameras were not digital like many of today's cameras. Negatives exposed in space came back to earth in film return capsules to be developed and studied.

Place Card 1 in front of the Hexagon Satellite in the
National Museum of the US Air Force
(Photo by Jessica L. Davis)

SATELLITES ON DISPLAY

In this gallery you will find three satellites: GAMBIT 1 KH-7, GAMBIT 3 KH-8, and HEXAGON KH-9. "KH" refers to the "Keyhole" code name for satellite camera systems. All three used specially-designed film and cameras to take pictures in orbit.

The vehicles on display are among the most important US photo reconnaissance systems used from the 1960s to the 1980s. The National Museum of the US Air Force wishes to thank the National Reconnaissance Office for loaning these significant satellites to the Museum.

Place Card 2 in front of the Hexagon Satellite in the
National Museum of the US Air Force
(Photo by Jessica L. Davis)

Lloyd Spanberger presenting in front of the Hexagon
Qualification Model in the National Museum of the US
Air Force on 26 January 2012 (Photo by Jessica Davis)

DORIAN

Prior to development of the Hexagon system, work began on the
Dorian (KH-10) manned reconnaissance system. The Dorian program was
the classified version of the Manned Orbiting Laboratory (MOL) program.
A modified Gemini-B capsule was to be used as the main spacecraft
and Eastman Kodak was to be the prime camera contractor. In reality,
there never was a serious MOL program. It was simply a cover program
for Dorian. As part of this cover, high school and university students
were offered the opportunity to submit experiments to be flown on the
vehicle. There were even contests to determine what projects would be
accepted, etc. Apparently, this cover approach worked quite well, since

several historical documents still represent this program to be a civilian space science project. The prime contractor had a separate facility for public viewing and tours of the satellite itself, however this was for show only and the public never knew what was really going on. The good news is the students learned a lot about working in space, in the process, so not all was a total loss.

The Dorian satellite was to have astronauts operate the camera system over select targets, in the hopes of detecting special classified characteristics of those targets. In short and simply put, they were looking for unique features worth documenting, for intelligence purposes. It turns out the computer system on board the Dorian satellite was programmed to select a known set of targets, similar to the Gambit system, and the astronaut operator only had a vote, as to whether or not to actually take the picture. Depending on cloud cover, etc, the computer could override the human operator. Due to the high resolution planned for the system, the astronauts only had about six seconds to decide whether the shot was worth taking, which made training an extremely important matter.

The R&D Directorate of AFSPPF was intimately involved in the development of Astronaut training techniques, in a technical consulting roll. Many coordination meetings were hosted and chaired by our facility regarding the aspects of this program. Multiple human factor problems were addressed, which were quite intriguing at that time. One in particular, without going into detail, was how to overcome the multiple tasks an astronaut had to accomplish at the same time. I recall a specific meeting where the concept of a mental control method was discussed. A couple of Astronauts and a Space Flight Surgeon were in attendance, whereby the test results were presented. It actually worked. The astronauts were wired up and simply (well, maybe not so simply) had to think about controlling switches and it happened. It was only on/off switch control, but that was exciting stuff at the time. Reliability was a serious consideration, if the technique were to eventually become operational, as one could imagine. I have no idea how far this concept progressed.

Ultimately, it was decided that Dorian was a bit too complicated and not cost effective and the program was cancelled. Although the Dorian mission was very specific, it was decided it could be accomplished with the Hexagon satellite, as well, without needing to support people in space.

AIRCRAFT

Aircraft reconnaissance support was primarily with the **U-2** and **SR-71** spy planes. We processed original negative and duplicate positive film for the U-2 and a limited amount for the SR-71.

U-2

It was sometime in early 1962 and our facility was firmly in the business of duplicating imagery from the Corona Satellite. One of our Alumni, who served in the Technical Analysis Division of our facility, told us a story, related to him, about one of our Airmen, who worked as a PI in the Analysis Section, at that time. He was looking at imagery over Cuba and noticed a change in the length of a steel span building. He observed, over several Corona missions, that the building was starting to grow in length. He brought this up to his supervisor, who initially dismissed it as no big deal. In later missions, he noticed it was still growing and had grown to around four times its original length. He thought this was a bit strange and brought it up to his supervisor once again. This time it was treated seriously and got reported to the CIA. The analysis was that the building was now long enough to hide a large missile. We have no direct knowledge of the chain of events that followed this reporting but we believe it significantly encouraged the CIA to look further. Although Corona imagery provided a clue of something significant developing, it is presumed that President Kennedy could not wait for additional satellite reconnaissance to find out what was happening, on a short-term basis. The analysis of satellite imagery was always a few weeks behind what was really going on. Aircraft imagery could be taken and analyzed within a day or so and provided much better resolution, although it was far riskier to obtain.

On the morning of October 14, 1962, a U-2 was called upon to fly over Cuba, as a pioneering flight, not by the CIA, but the USAF representing the DOD. Major Richard Heyser of the 4080th SRW (Strategic Reconnaissance Wing) at Del Rio, Texas, was handed a CIA U-2C aircraft at Edwards AFB, California, and flew across Western Cuba that same day. Upon completion of his mission, he landed at McCoy AFB (now known as Orlando International Airport), Florida. In the days to follow, multiple U-2 flights were flown from McCoy AFB and several from Laughlin AFB, Del Rio, TX. Within ten days or so, the entire island was photographed and the full extent of the problem was identified. Ultimately, by sometime in early November 1962, all follow on U-2 flights were flown from Laughlin AFB under Operation "Brass Knob".

There is considerable conjecture and rumors floating around that our facility processed film from that first flight on October 14th. The people, who knew the facts, have now passed away and we have not been able to verify, without question, that this is true. We believe it to be more likely the film from the first flight was processed at a naval facility (NRTSC - Naval Reconnaissance Technical Support Center) in Suitland, MD, just outside Washington DC. However, we did process original negative film from subsequent U-2 flights during the weeks following the historic October 14 mission. According to our lab people, once the film was processed, it was immediately packaged up and sent out. We believe NPIC was the destination. We also know other processing laboratories, including SAC HQ at Offutt AFB, were involved in this effort, but we have no idea to what extent.

AFSPPF had a secondary mission as a backup to NRTSC in support of their duties to process certain U-2 missions. We maintained technical liaison with NRTSC and processed at least one complete U-2 mission (O/N's and Dup Positives) while they were down for facility modifications.

One of our Alumni, former CMSgt William (Bill) Ray, was the NCOIC of the photo lab, at that time, and has submitted his story of our involvement, as best he can recall. Bill served in the Production Directorate of our facility from 1961 to 1971. The following is his story, presented in his own words:

"This is what I can remember about the Cuban Missile Crisis, pertaining to the processing of original negative film. I was the NCOIC of the film-processing unit.

The product was processed in the HTA3 processor. These machines had been modified with spray nozzles and dry sumps. They were located in a temporary location near the South East corner of the building, while a place was being constructed for them in the clean room.

I cannot pinpoint the exact day of the crisis that the product showed up at our facility for processing. We processed the original negatives and it was shipped out immediately. I do not think the product was in the building over two hours. From that time on, we processed the U-2 imagery, concerning the Crisis, every day, until it was over.

I have no knowledge of the person or persons who designated the product be shipped to us for processing or who was the receiver of the finished product.

When the awards and decorations were being passed around, for participation in the Crisis, our unit was a non-receiver. Later, the Air Force Outstanding Unit Award was awarded to us."

SR-71

Primary support for the SR-71 was provided by our associated units overseas, although our facility did its fair share of photo development for this aircraft. See Chapter 10, for a description of those units. It was recalled that our facility supported the testing of photo systems for the SR-71 in the 1964-65 period. Apparently, there were problems with visual imaging through a hot window, causing some optical distortion. We, at least, did our part and, eventually, it all worked out. At most, the distortion affected the quality of the final image, but it got through to the film.

We also provided technical support to the 9 RTS at Beale AFB. Our people spent a full week there, in the fall of 1968, showing them how to implement Low Gamma processing for an extended range development process they were beginning to use. The AFSPPF developed initial Low and Dual Gamma processing technology in this time frame. Not only did EK embrace the technology, but other manufactures, e.g. Itek G4L and Hunt Chemical Hunts ER (extended range), did, as well.

Although not directly connected to AFSPPF, the following story may be of interest and is included as a side note, since it may have resulted in my assignment to the facility, which I suspect but cannot verify.

Prior to my assignment to AFSPPF, I was assigned to the Air Force Infrared Reconnaissance Lab at Wright Patterson AFB, as a research physicist. While there, I ran a three-year program (1963 to 1966) on the X-15 aircraft to prove the viability of IR imaging in a SR-71 environment. I also observed that visual camera systems were also being tested on the X-15, during this time. Apparently, our facility processed film from several of these missions. Use of the SR-71, itself, was not possible then, due to its early stage of development. Many problems had to be solved, including development of a new IR window material (Kodak IRTRAN IV, Zinc Selenide) and a method to produce it in large enough segments suitable for installation and use with the IR imaging scanner, provided by the HRB Singer Corp. The purpose of this development effort was to solve the unique problems in making IR reconnaissance operational in the SR-71.

As with visual reconnaissance, in this environment, successful IR imaging through a hot window was a huge concern. The IR scanner looked in the 8-14 micron region of the electromagnetic spectrum, which required the use of super cooled sensors. Liquid Neon was used as the coolant for this program and was held in a specially designed container called a Dewar (similar to a standard vacuum bottle). Loading liquid Neon into the Dewar, just before flight, was a serious problem. Due to its rapid evaporation tendencies, it had to be done then or it wouldn't last long enough to complete the mission. The X-15 pre-flight checklist had to be modified to allow access to the equipment just before the B-52 mother ship took off with it. This situation became a political, as well as a technical problem. The political problem was the biggest, but was eventually solved and a hatch was installed to allow the access we needed, when we needed it. The other major problem was keeping the liquid Neon inside the Dewar under zero and negative G conditions, which were to be experienced during the flight profile. This extremely cold liquid wanted to just jump out of the Dewar under these conditions, so an internal stainless steel mesh had to be designed to help hold it in. Ultimately, it worked and we succeeded. Fortunately, all these problems were anticipated in advance, which greatly contributed to success on the first flight. The signals generated by the IR sensor had to be converted to visible light and finally recorded onto photographic film, during the actual mission.

Ultimately, the concept was proven at speeds of Mach 5 at 100 thousand feet in altitude (Far more extreme than the SR-71 flight profile), and we could image through a hot window and look right through the boundary layer generated by a supersonic aircraft. This work was in support of SR-71 project "Blue Feather" and resulted in the solution of the hot window and other problems associated with IR imaging in this hostile environment. The following image shows the IR window installed in the X-15. It had to be constructed in three segments, due to manufacturing limitations at that time. This photo is provided from my personal records.

IR window mounted in the belly of the X-15
(Photo by Lloyd R. Spanberger)

Infrared imagery was meant to show a reasonable amount of resolution, but primarily to show activity, such as operating power plants, radar sites, underground structures generating heat, etc. It was quite valuable when used in conjunction with visual photography as well as independent nighttime reconnaissance. Ultimately, for whatever reason, I believe some version of a Synthetic Aperture Radar (SAR) replaced the IR system, in the SR-71, in the early 1970s.

As an additional side note, it turns out this program was the most successful program ever run on the X-15 aircraft, or so I was told by the Airplane Manager. We were the only program that got data on our very first flight. Furthermore, we got good data on the next three flights, before total equipment failure on flight five. Flight six was successful and the program concluded. The bugs were all worked out and we had a proven plan to make IR reconnaissance operational in this extreme environment.

At this point, my involvement was over. Interestingly, Col. Ralph Swofford, who was the SR-71 SPO (System Program Office) Commander, during this time, eventually became the Deputy Commander of AFSPPF while I was assigned to the facility. Both visual and IR programs were run on the X-15 Aircraft #1, which is now hanging in the Smithsonian Air and Space Museum, in Washington DC (without the IR window).

Tagboard Drone

There was a brief period when the Mach 3 supersonic Tagboard Drone (D-21) was operational. It is generally known what the U-2 and SR-71 aircraft were. The Tagboard drone, however, was an aircraft similar to the SR-71 in performance and was used briefly during the late 1960s and early 1970s. It was, obviously, unmanned and originally designed to be launched from a special two seat version of the A-12 Oxcart (early version of the SR-71), designated M-21. "M" designated "Mother" and "D" designated "Daughter". Doing so was a particularly difficult task and, after several narrow escapes and problems, including the eventual loss of an M-21 and D-21 during a collision at launch, along with one crewmember, the D-21 was modified for launch from a B-52, similar to how the X-15 rocket plane was launched. These modified versions were designated D-21B and included disposable rocket boosters to get them up to speed before the Ram Jets kicked in. Launch from YF-12s didn't require boosters, since they were already traveling at Mach 3 plus.

Each Tagboard drone was programmed to fly a specific course over enemy territory and photograph designated targets, very similar to the SR-71 missions. Upon completion of its mission, the drone would return to a safe area, over water, whereby it would drop its film bucket for midair pickup by a specially equipped Air Force plane. The technique used was pretty much the same as that used to snatch film buckets from satellites. Should the plane miss, the bucket would float until it could be picked up by an appropriate naval vessel. The film bucket would then be taken to a suitable processing facility for development, duplication and analysis. There was no intent to recover the drone, itself. AFSPPF personnel processed film from two of the few operational missions actually flown with this drone. Images of all these aircraft are shown below.

U-2 (US Air Force Photo)

SR-71 (US Air Force Photo)

D-21 Tagboard Drone on a YF-12
(US Air Force Photo)

D-21 Tagboard Drone on a YF-12
(CIA photo)

Twin Tagboard Drones on a B-52
(US Air Force Photo)

Tagboard Drone on a B-52 (Close Up)
(US Air Force Photo)

Miscellaneous Organizations

Our facility was also secretly mandated to provide personnel, material, equipment procurement and technical assistance for discrete and covert overseas organizations with DOD directed aerial reconnaissance and intelligence collection activities. Almost all this support was off the books. Personnel were supplied via TDY (Temporary Duty) and PCS (Permanent change of station) means. Virtually no documentation is available to tell this story and, most probably, will never be found. It is doubtful it ever existed and, if it did, it no longer does. Normal Air Force administrative and procurement channels were bypassed. The standing policy was "Do what it takes to get the job done". See Chapter 10 for more detail on these overseas organizations supported.

Processing flow for film buckets dropped from satellites & Tagboard Drones

The following diagrams (Developed by Al Crane) depict the general path of the film, once dropped from their respective satellites. Although AFSPPF processed duplicate imagery from all Corona missions, it is noted that the last three Corona missions were totally processed (O/N's and Duplicate Positives) and distributed by AFSPPF. As can be seen, Kodak Bridgehead processed the original negatives from the majority of the Corona and Gambit missions. Original negatives from Hexagon were processed by Perkin Elmer (PE) and Kodak, Bridgehead.

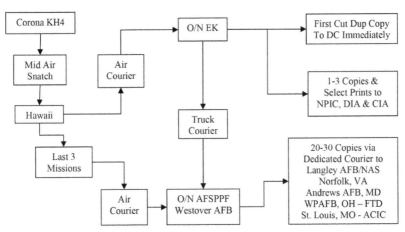

Corona film bucket and image process, duplication and distribution flow

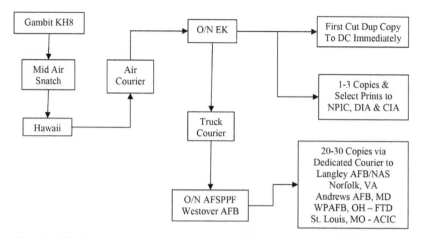

Gambit film bucket and image process, duplication and distribution flow

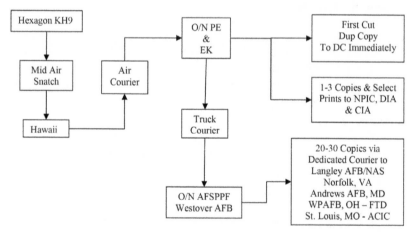

Hexagon film bucket and image process, duplication and distribution flow

The large courier missions depicted here were the typical 'MINIBALL' missions mentioned earlier. In reality, there were many other diverse delivery missions, to a variety of intelligence organizations.

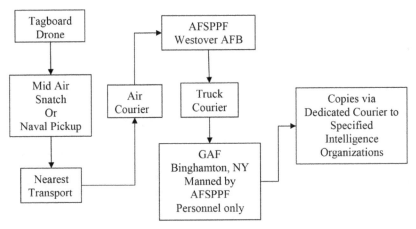

**Tagboard Drone film bucket and image process/duplication
and distribution flow**

Note that the film bucket, from the Tagboard Drone, was to be picked up by naval vessels, should the mid air snatch fail to happen. The bucket was then transported to AFSPPF who, in turn, took it to GAF Corporation, where AFSPPF personnel used their equipment to develop and duplicate the onboard film for distribution.

(Al Crane was one of a select few individuals involved with the Tagboard Drone film processing effort. He recalls the following circumstances with two successful missions of the program, that we know of.)

Special Tagboard Drone Missions

"We processed two missions, both over China. The film used was GAF ASA 400 color film. According to the NRO, the higher ASA was required to compensate for the low light level from the target scene received at the Tagboard sensor, due to the altitude and speed of the vehicle and aperture of the sensor. The Kodak ASA 64 color film was unacceptable for use in this environment.

Our first mission was processed in-house by SMSgt "Moose" Miller and me. Since the film was incompatible with the Kodak Color Versamat continuous film processor, it was processed on an old style manual reel-to-reel processor (believed to be Korean War era). It turns out that GAF neglected to inform us about the need to use Gantrez (a proprietary GAF lubricant) for manual reel-to-reel processing of long rolls of film, prior to the final drying phase. The result was a disaster, since the emulsion separated from the film base and the imagery was destroyed. Needless to say, it was a bad day all around. This incident clearly points out the importance of a well functioning film-processing lab in the grand scheme of things. Imagine the extent of the loss in equipment, resources, manpower and money all because of a simple glitch in film processing. This was an extremely rare and devastating event for our facility.

Prior to processing the first mission film we received, we mixed the GAF processing chemicals and subjected them to the highest QC tests, such as, PH, traces of contamination and temperature. We ran a series of short rolls of Sensitometric and color patch test strips on exposed GAF film and analyzed the H&D curves, color fidelity, etc. All met specifications. There was absolutely no indication that emulsion separation would occur.

The processing unit was meticulously cleaned and checked for any malfunctions & contaminants present. Processing was conducted in the clean room with SMSgt Miller and me, fully dressed in "Bunny Suits", to preclude any external contamination.

Only when we processed the mission film did we experience the emulsion separation on the roll (as I recall, about 100-200 ft of film). It was well after the fact that we learned of the GANTREX lubricant requirement, which was not included in the "normal" processing chemical package.

Things were very different the next time. So as to not have a repeat performance and just in case there were other tidbits of information left out of the processing requirements, it was decided to "Rent" the GAF facility, in Binghamton, NY, for the next mission and use their continuous roll processing machines optimized for ASA 400 film. Col Swofford took a team of our personnel to the GAF plant to process the second mission. Once GAF technicians put our people through a thorough familiarization process on their equipment, they were cleared out of the facility and our people completed the processing task. This mission was successful and, after a standard evaluation at AFSPPF, I, along with another officer, couriered the film to Los Angeles via a commercial flight. We delivered it to a designated courier from the CIA at Los Angeles International Airport (LAX). We have no idea what happened to the film after that. Our job was finished and we returned to AFSPPF.

It is interesting to note that the ASA 400 film was later used by the US Navy for water penetration experiments, since it was optimized for the task due to a blue light sensitive layer. During the later days of the Vietnam War, while I was stationed in the Pentagon as the USAF Photo Staff Officer, we were directed to evaluate the use of this film to aid in underwater mine detection missions along the Mekong River. The missions were indirectly successful. Due to the murky water in the Mekong River, we were not able to achieve water penetration to detect the mines directly. However, the Photo Interpreters were able to detect the "V" wakes from the suspended mines and this secondary signature allowed us to plot their locations."

CHAPTER 8

Personal Recollections of CMSgt Jim Grimm (ret.)

This entire chapter was contributed by James (Jim) O. Grimm.

Manning and Assignment Authority

"The facility possessed DOD authority to recruit any qualified Air Force person from any location, worldwide, for assignment to the facility. Assignment was based on rank, job code and security clearance. Once assigned to the facility, the assignment became permanent. The only break in this policy was during the Vietnam War, when personnel could be shipped to South East Asia and then returned to the facility upon completion of their overseas tour, unless an individual rejected re-assignment to the facility. Additionally, a former facility person could bypass the facility by requesting assignment to one of the related overseas locations. In addition, personnel, in facility connected overseas locations, if sent to South East Asia, could return to their previous overseas location, bypassing the USA.

Massive recruitment was periodically done at the USAF Training Command Precision Processing School, at Lowry AFB, CO. Recruits were interviewed and selected based on personality traits, ability to obtain a security clearance and academic records. After graduation, selected personnel records were submitted to USAF Personnel Assignment Headquarters for direct assignment to the facility. Individual personnel selections were secretly made in many ways without obtaining approval through USAF Personnel Assignment Headquarters. Selection was mainly done through private correspondence and telephone calls between a responsible individual at the facility, or at one of its overseas units, and the individual desiring assignment to the facility, or related overseas unit. Once an individual's credentials were approved by the facility or related overseas unit, arrangements were made through USAF Personnel Assignment Headquarters to have the selected individual reassigned. Selections were based on rank, skill level, advanced technical training, security clearance and job classification codes. The facility, and any related overseas unit, had priority and authority to request, via USAF Personnel Assignment Headquarters, changes in assignment of personnel who were in the re-assignment pipeline and whose qualifications were found to be advantageous to the facility or overseas unit.

Summary of Laboratory Operation

Creation of the AFSPPF Laboratory

The AFSPPF laboratory was established as a Top Secret Air Force (USAF) "backup" facility to the Kodak Hawkeye Plant (Bridgehead) in Rochester, NY. Bridgehead's Government Top Secret contract included precision photo processing and production of high altitude imagery collected from U-2, SR-71 and spy satellite platforms.

Generally, Kodak processed the "original" imagery (also known as O/N – Original Negative) and made a "master" duplicate negative copy for ground transportation to the AFSPPF, which then used it to produce additional duplicate positive "working" copies for use by the intelligence community. Transportation was via armed couriers in locked unmarked trucks with special Department of Transportation authority. The AFSPPF was considered the "workhorse" for the production of duplicate Top Secret imagery for Cold War intelligence exploitation and reporting.

The AFSPPF laboratory was designed and personnel trained to completely back up Bridgehead for original and duplicate processing of any type of intelligence imagery collected from high altitude platforms, in black and white or color. With the existence of the AFSPPF, Kodak's Bridgehead activity was completely backed up in case their laboratory encountered production problems. Processing of original imagery collected by spy aircraft and satellites was always of urgent priority and could not be delayed.

In addition to maintaining an O/N and duplicate imagery processing capability, the AFSPPF laboratory was chartered to support USAF research and development objectives necessary to enhance laboratory operational procedures and improve equipment designs.

AFSPPF Production Directorate

The AFSPPF Production Directorate included three Divisions; namely, Production, Quality Control (QC), and Computer Support, which, together, formed the nucleus of the AFSPPF laboratory. These three divisions were widely known as the "USAF Cold War Leaders" in planning, developing, and implementing advanced precision photo processing, reproduction, and QC methodologies; thus, enabling the directorate to contribute significantly to the success of AFSPPF, USAF, DOD and other Government agencies in intelligence collection, processing, and exploitation programs, during the Cold War.

Without joint application and integration of precision photo processing, QC, and computer support efficiencies, successful production of vital intelligence imagery was impossible. These three divisions, working together in a dust-free clean room environment, made it possible for the Government to launch multi-million dollar high altitude reconnaissance missions, and have a high degree of confidence in the ultimate production of superior intelligence products. Processed imagery required optimum resolution and finite detail without any type of degradation, to be of optimum value to the end user.

There were myriad technical phases and details required in the production of intelligence imagery, especially from spy satellite platforms. Therefore, to prevent the reader/layman from falling asleep while reading this article, many boring technical details have been eliminated.

Functional Responsibilities

The photo processing activity was responsible for chemistry preparation and distribution, printer and processor operations, cleaning and annotation of imagery, administrative control of production flow, calibration and certification of production equipment and housekeeping of clean room facilities.

The QC activity was responsible for analysis of chemistry, inspection of imagery for proper tonal ranges prior to and after production, release of finished products for shipment, calibration and certification of quality control equipment, and monitoring and reporting of processing, printing, product quality and clean room operating parameters.

The computer support activity was responsible for tracking each product through different phases of production. Issuance of timely computer reports for management perusal included number of products completed, defective units, location of each product in the production flow, and other quality assurance data regarding original and duplicate imagery inspections.

Photo Science and Engineering Training

Flawless processing of irreplaceable intelligence imagery was made possible through application of photo sciences and engineering concepts. Personnel assigned to the Production Directorate were academically trained to achieve the best product possible, using the most intricate and sophisticated multi-million dollar spy satellite laboratory, support systems and materials. All laboratory production, quality control, and management personnel were graduates of the USAF Training Command's Precision Photo Processing School at Lowry AFB, CO. Photo science and engineering courses taught at the school were developed by Rochester Institute of Technology and Massachusetts Institute of Technology.

The photo science and engineering curriculum also included use of the now forgotten "slide rule" (For those too young to know about such a device, a slide rule was the mechanical version of an electronic hand held calculator), which was extensively used by senior laboratory management for calculating statistical data.

To ensure standardization and technical continuity in laboratory operations between Kodak's Bridgehead and AFSPPF, occasionally, there was an exchange of certain personnel between these two organizations. During selected missions, the AFSPPF temporarily transferred a limited number of laboratory personnel to Bridgehead to work with Kodak technicians. To reciprocate, Bridgehead transferred certain technicians to the AFSPPF. This procedure ensured that both entities were on the same page, technically, for processing and production of intelligence imagery.

These technician transfers were secret and not discussed with other personnel outside of laboratory operations in either organization. These temporary assignments were strictly on a need to know basis.

Noteworthy, in the advanced education area, the AFSPPF laboratory's personnel manning document authorized two graduate chemists with advanced knowledge in photochemistry. These chemists managed the laboratory's chemical analysis function, which was often required to change the formulation and ingredient balance of chemistry to meet demanding research requirements of certain agencies supported by the facility.

Overview of Laboratory Activities

Laboratory activities were labor-intensive and functioned, as previously mentioned, in a computer monitored and controlled clean room environment. The combined precision photo processing, QC and computer activities formed the largest group within the AFSPPF with approximately 135 technicians and management personnel assigned. Twelve-hour shifts were used in a continuous mode (24/7) basis until each mission was completed.

A special data monitoring system, usually manned by QC personnel, was used to monitor particle count, airflow, clean room temperature and humidity, and online processor control parameters. Utility support for the laboratory was also monitored and displayed on a large control panel located near the data monitoring system.

Computerized production monitoring systems were used to track products through various phases of processing, reproduction, QC and shipping cycles. Production and QC reports were timely generated for management review.

To prevent contamination in the clean room, a continuous positive airflow was essential. Personnel were required to wear lint-free, white bunny suits, masks, caps, boots, and gloves and to step on "tacky mats", prior to proceeding through air showers and entry into secured work areas. Anything, including pencils and standard writing paper, causing airborne dust particles was prohibited in the clean room. To help enforce this restriction, bunny suits contained no pockets for personal items. Equipment and workbenches were made of non-static producing stainless steel and kept polished with a special cleaning solution.

Laboratory operations were conducted according to AFSPPF certified operational standards. Each product produced was critically evaluated and approved by QC technicians using special image analysis systems, prior to shipment.

Unique processing, reproduction, and QC systems included original and duplicate film processors, pre-inspection pre-splice tables, high resolution printers, titlers, and various types of image quality measuring systems such as microscopes, manual and auto densitometers, editing tables and sensitometers.

The sensitometer was an intricate tool used to produce test materials for controlling processors and testing of chemistry. The densitometer was a precision measuring tool used to read the processed test materials produced by the sensitometer. Densitometers were also used to measure and control image quality.

A large "tank farm" providing specially prepared certified chemistry to processors 24/7, was about 5000 square feet in size, and used stainless steel mixers and storage tanks with 1500-2500 gallon capacities. Chemistry was precisely mixed according to written operating procedures and distributed from storage tanks to processors via a sophisticated control panel and stainless steel pipes. Intercom systems were used to coordinate accurate and timely flow of chemistry from tank farm to processors. The tank farm, for safety reasons and due to use of highly caustic chemicals, was always manned by at least two technicians wearing appropriate safety gear.

A complete chemical analysis function supervised by two graduate chemists was in operation 24/7 to conduct testing and certification of different types of chemistry used in the laboratory.

Laboratory Certification Process

Before original or duplicate film processing operations could begin, it was mandatory that all laboratory functions be fully certified to produce the highest quality product possible.

Hours of thorough processor testing included the processing of special test materials to verify proper processor speed, replenishment rates, and chemistry quality. Mechanical readiness of the processor included elimination of tracking problems, foreign particles and ineffective squeegee and drying system problems. Printing equipment was required to go through a similar process. Printer and processor certification was tedious and closely monitored and approved by designated QC technicians. Final approval sometimes required 2 to 3 days, working 24/7, until all problems were resolved and QC standards were met.

While printer and processor certifications were being accomplished, all QC equipment and certain other types of production systems were simultaneously subjected to their own certification procedures. Included were film titlers, film cleaners, manual and automatic digital densitometers, power driven densitometer tables, and imagery editing systems (There were occasions when certain highly sensitive images had to be deleted, not duplicated or designated for specific customers only. There were very few lab personnel cleared for this activity).

After the laboratory was completely certified and approved to begin O/N or duplicate imagery processing operations, the printers and processors remained in continuous operation, 24/7, until a project or mission was completed, sometimes 2 to 3 weeks. Online systems were kept in control by QC technicians who constantly monitored relevant data to ensure systems operating standards were met.

Maintaining the Trenton O/N processor in optimum control was critical because of the irreplaceable imagery being processed. The Dalton duplicate positive processors could fail without causing a severe impact to mission accomplishment, since the duplicate imagery being processed could be reprinted again in the laboratory. This procedure was impossible with original imagery produced by aircraft or satellite cameras.

One final comment about the laboratory certification process: AFSPPF Maintenance Division personnel deserve credit for their demonstrated technical performance in maintaining laboratory systems in a high state of operational readiness. Their expertise in preventive and repair maintenance eliminated long periods of systems downtime and made certification of the laboratory much easier.

AFSPPF Processing of Original Imagery

Original film from aircraft or satellite platforms, when directly received at the AFSPPF for processing, instead of Kodak's Bridgehead, was carefully removed, in a totally dark environment, from protective containers commonly known as "buckets" (about the size of a typical garbage container). The film was inspected for physical defects via use of a pre-inspection and splicing table and mobile dolly, and repaired and spliced if necessary. The dolly was then attached to a certified O/N Trenton processor. Preparing the unprocessed film for attachment to the Trenton was tedious and could take hours. In order to appreciate the quality and uniqueness of the people working with this processor, try doing anything in a totally dark environment for any length of time to get a feel for the difficulty of this process.

The Trenton processor was exceptionally large and was equipped with an infrared viewing station, which enabled a technician to view progress of the imagery being processed without affecting the development of the film itself. If the development process needed adjustment, the technician could manually increase or decrease development rates to achieve an improved image. Intervention of the development process required the experience of a well-seasoned technician, keeping in mind that Trenton processor technicians were dealing with irreplaceable intelligence imagery.

Processing time, for an original mission could take 2 to 3 days, depending on the length of the film. Operating the complex O/N processor efficiently, required a minimum of five highly trained technicians and one supervisor, 24/7, until the mission was complete.

Processed film, as it came off the processor, was cut into manageable lengths and critically inspected for defects and overall quality. Mission quality control reports were then generated for management review.

Production of Duplicate Imagery

Original imagery was accurately titled via sophisticated titling machines and prepared for duplication as required, which included precise tonal range measurements and issuance of written instructions for printer technicians who used special Niagara printers to produce a duplicate negative master from the original imagery.

Noteworthy, is that original imagery was never used to produce working copy duplicate positives for the intelligence community. Irreplaceable original imagery was preserved for Top Secret intelligence archival use only. Once the duplicate negatives masters were made, the originals were shipped to NPIC for storage.

The duplicate negative masters were also inspected by QC technicians for physical defects and tonal range variances. Printing instructions were then issued to make duplicate positive working copies. These copies were produced on a hi-speed Dalton processor, generally manned by at least three technicians. The printing and processing of duplicate positives was performed in a low-level red light environment. This was possible, since the duplicate film was not sensitive to red light. This made for a much more comfortable work environment.

The duplicate negative masters, produced in Kodak's Bridgehead facility, were inspected and treated exactly as though they were produced within AFSPPF. They were then used to make duplicate positives for designated customers. The majority of duplicate master negative copies came from the Bridgehead facility.

The AFSPPF laboratory developed and used a proprietary Tri-Gradient printing and processing system to produce the highest image quality possible, especially when original imagery was exposed during bad weather conditions. This system was based on mathematical calculations of image density ranges and then selecting the proper processing curve (low, medium or high gamma) to transform as much of the total image range, in the negative, to where the human eye could see the whole thing in the duplicate positive. This technique was eventually adopted for use by precision photo processing laboratories throughout the USAF.

AFSPPF eventually went to a single dual gamma processing technique, pioneered and developed in house, using wet chemical techniques, versus a much more expensive and toxic viscous technique developed by Kodak.

AFSPPF saved the Air Force hundreds of thousands of dollars with this approach and, as usual, there was no recognition of this accomplishment. The dual gamma technique accomplished the same results as the Tri-Gradient approach, without the need to figure out which processing curve to use. All this seems so simple now after all these years, but at the time; it was new and innovative and produced excellent results. Although the Tri-Gradient approach became the standard for other Air Force processing labs, dual gamma did not. It was apparently too complicated a process to be used beyond the AFSPPF and Bridgehead class of operations.

Duplicate imagery produced in the laboratory was inspected for physical degradation, proper tonal range, resolution and overall image quality. If proper QC standards were met, the finished product was placed on an underground conveyor belt and sent to the Shipping Department for packaging and additional documentation.

A famous humorous statement by QC technicians; "if you can see a person on the ground riding a bicycle, then acceptable image quality from extremely high altitude camera systems has been achieved." "Ship it!"

Mission Completion

After a mission was completed, the laboratory was completely scrubbed and sanitized for classified material. Preventive maintenance was performed to ensure the highest state of operational readiness for the next mission or project. The laboratory NCOIC and one other senior person thoroughly inspected the laboratory after each mission. Any discrepancies were immediately corrected.

Production Statistics

Approximately 15 years of spy satellite support resulted in processing and production of over 800,000 images, or a total of 2.1 million feet of film.

Laboratory Special Projects & Achievements

The precision processing laboratory, with highly trained technicians, and multi-million dollar intelligence imagery processing and production systems, was also a "Test Bed" for the USAF and other Government intelligence agencies for advancing the state-of-the-art in intelligence imagery collection platforms, and continued improvement in precision processing and production technologies. Specific accomplishments were as follows:

- Special imagery processing, production, and quality control procedures and equipment designs were developed for ultimate use throughout the USAF and by other Government intelligence producing agencies.
- Initiated manufacturing requirement and assisted manufacturer in design of the digital densitometer to replace the obsolete analog type used in industry. Using a digital display was much more user friendly and eliminated any possibility of operator error.
- Initiated manufacturing requirement and assisted manufacturer in design of improved processor air impingement and squeegee drier systems to increase film-processing speeds and improve image quality by elimination of water spotting.
- Initiated manufacturing requirement for self-sealing durable plastic film containers versus metal containers which created contamination in a clean room environment.
- Initiated manufacturing requirement for 1200 ft (versus 500 ft) rolls of duplicating film, which improved the efficiency of the high-speed printers. This saved the technician much time and increased production. These containers were eventually used throughout the USAF.
- As previously mentioned, the laboratory developed a proprietary Tri-Gradient image tone control system used to manipulate the printing and wet processing phase required to improve exploitation quality of the product. This system was incorporated into Air Force Training Command Manuals for use throughout other USAF precision photo processing units.
- Periodically, experienced laboratory specialists were secretly dispatched to other USAF units to train technicians on the proper use of Tri-Gradient image processing technology, in order to decrease the high cost of precision photo processing chemistry, and to enhance the quality of irreplaceable imagery taken over denied territories.
- A proprietary developer was developed and produced from bulk chemicals, versus the costly purchase of pre-packaged ready-to-use chemicals. Over many years of operation, in-house preparation of this chemistry saved hundreds of thousands of dollars, while simultaneously producing a product of significantly higher quality.
- The Photo Lab and Quality Control frequently tested and evaluated many different types of imagery processing and reproduction systems and materials for potential use throughout the USAF, and other research organizations, including universities, and Government agencies.

Unique Laboratory Systems for Spy Aircraft and Satellites

AFSPPF and Kodak's Bridgehead were the only organizations possessing a complete inventory of unique state-of-the-art production and test equipment, skill levels, and clean room environment required to effectively process and reproduce high-resolution images collected by spy aircraft and satellites.

Production and QC systems were costly and required technically educated personnel to operate with a high degree of confidence. Otherwise, Top Secret irreplaceable intelligence imagery could be severely damaged during processing, or totally lost due to operator error.

Following are pictures of some of the multi-million dollar major systems used at the AFSPPF. Procurement source was generally Kodak's Hawkeye Plant, which not only designed elaborate reconnaissance support systems for the Government, but also because of complexity in operation of the systems, was also responsible for initial installation and training of technicians.

Laboratory Production Systems

The following photographs show the various equipments and facilities related to the Photo Lab.

AFSPPF Chemical Hoppers and Mixing Tanks
(US Air Force Photo)

AFSPPF Stainless Steel Solution Storage Tanks
(US Air Force Photo)

AFSPPF Chemical Mix Tank Farm (US Air Force Photo)

AFSPPF Chemical Mix Tanks (US Air Force Photo)

AFSPPF Chemical Mix Control and Distribution Panel
(US Air Force Photo)

Partial View of Support Plumbing for the Trenton
Original Negative Film Processor
(US Air Force Photo)

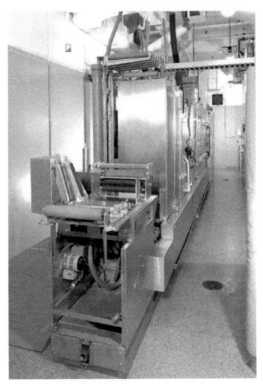

Trenton Original Negative Film Processor
(Photo used with permission of Eastman Kodak Company)

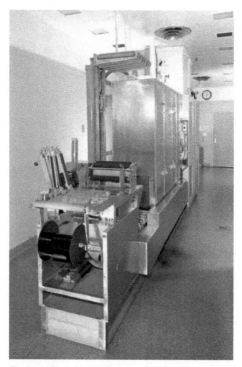

Dalton Duplicate Imagery Film Processor
(Photo used with permission of Eastman Kodak Company)

Niagara Printer
(Photo used with permission of Eastman Kodak Company)

Dual Head Film Titler
(Photo used with permission of Eastman Kodak Company)

Bill Dishon in a Clean Room Uniform without Mask
(US Air Force Photo)

Quality Control Systems

The following photographs show the various equipments and facilities related to the QC Div.

AFSPPF Data Monitoring Console (US Air Force Photo)

AFSPPF Data Monitoring Control Panel (US Air Force photo)

Densitometer Table, Model II, Motor Wind
(Used with permission of Eastman Kodak Company)

Microscope Viewing Table, Motor Wind
(Used with permission of Eastman Kodak Company)

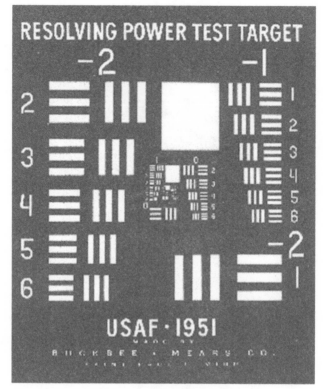

Resolution Test Target (US Air Force photo)

The preceding pictures of laboratory and QC systems in this article should help the reader understand product flow, processing and evaluation. Equipment was unique, customized, very expensive and generally limited to Kodak Bridgehead and AFSPPF laboratories.

Product flow was not fixed and was often changed to meet production requirements and quality control constraints.

During my four years (1963-1967) as NCOIC (non-commissioned officer in-charge) of the AFSPPF precision photo-processing laboratory, many technical challenges were encountered, but with outstanding performance of skilled technicians, mission effectiveness never wavered.

I will never forget when the laboratory was requested by one of the research agencies to urgently process a scientific test roll of film to a certain standard. As the processor was causing water spots during the certification cycle, the technicians ask me to assist in resolving the problem. I sent one of the technicians to buy a block of salt (a salt lick for cattle) and place it in the processor sump to soften the wash water. After another test run, the water spots disappeared, enabling the agency's scientific test to be processed without further delay. This method of eliminating water spots was not common and would not work under high production conditions, but it was a quick-fix for a problem that was labor-intensive and causing a backup in the production flow of other products.

Mission accomplishment required teamwork, organization, positive attitude, endurance, perseverance, exceptional skills, and a desire to win the Cold War.

Working 12-hour shifts in a continuous mode, while donned in clean room clothing, and working under strict deadlines to complete high priority intelligence missions, were factors that could cause psychological problems and adversely affect a person's ability to think clearly and to make critical technical decisions. Fortunately, personnel had the stamina and will power to endure these conditions. I remember one period when the workload was overwhelming and laboratory personnel worked 60 days straight, without a day off.

The reader must remember that, compared to civilian peers at Kodak Bridgehead, AFSPPF technicians were severely under paid for the same performance. In the military, there is no compensation for overtime worked and pay scales are much lower. Civilians at Bridgehead were on a corporate competitive pay scale and abundantly paid for work performed over eight hours in a day, and during weekends and holidays.

Laboratory technicians ending their career at AFSPPF, in many cases, were offered the same type of work at Bridgehead for much more compensation. This opportunity gave AFSPPF technicians something to think about after discharge from military service. In any case, with their security clearance, they were immediately employable, if they wanted to work for Bridgehead.

Personnel Quarters

Enlisted personnel quarters were located in a single location at a remote site away from the main base and in a somewhat desolate location. Personnel from other organizations were not co-mingled and quartered with facility personnel.

In-House Photo Engineering and Science Seminars

Advanced periodic RIT and MIT technology seminars were held in house for senior technicians, engineers and managers. Secret funding was sponsored by an unidentified intelligence agency. Attendance was limited to certain personnel who were adept in the areas of statistics and the scientific processing and reproduction of high-resolution satellite imagery.

Private Mail Boxes

Certain facility personnel possessed private mailboxes at unknown locations for hiding their identity. These boxes were used for receiving business mail from outside sources. False names and addresses were used to hide identity of the box holder. The Special Activities Office (SAO) maintained these boxes, which were used, among other reasons, to receive code words for courier duty, etc. Mail was always picked up while wearing civilian clothes. The SAO also maintained phone numbers with Washington DC numbers, to hide the source of communications, in certain circumstances.

Private Military Doctors

Select on-base doctors were briefed and limited to doctor-patient conversations. This policy was due to the exceptional stress and long working hours, which could adversely affect the behavior of a person and result in security leaks, during medical discussions with a doctor. Patients could not be asked unnecessary organizational or job-related questions.

Personnel Missing From Work

Personnel missing from work for more than two hours without notification of their status were put under alert and immediate search initiated. Fortunately, during my time as NCOIC of the laboratory, this problem never occurred. Personnel were advised to keep their supervisor informed of their whereabouts if they planned to be absent from work.

Personnel temporarily dispatched to overseas or other locations, to provide technical assistance, traveled "In Status," without being debriefed. If required, due to security conditions at the temporary location or during travel, Debriefing Statements were signed before departure in case of no return. Information about a person's temporary official absence from the AFSPPF was never discussed among associates, or with other operational components in the AFSPPF. Only military aircraft were appropriate when traveling to and from overseas locations.

A Final Note

Many thanks to all AFSPPF laboratory technicians who contributed significantly to helping the United States win the Cold War. The products they produced for the intelligence community were timely, of superior quality and invaluable to national security. In addition, our spouses and other family members, who felt the stress of long working hours, but never fully understood their partner's military duties because of security constraints, definitely deserve acknowledgment for their perseverance and understanding."

CHAPTER 9

Mr. George J. Myers –
Historical Summary

The following historical summary was written by Mr. George J. Myers, who served as the civilian Technical Director of AFSPPF from 1967–1976, just prior to his passing in the summer of 2012. He was not, therefore, able to attend our brainstorming sessions at our October 2012 reunion, whereby we collectively attempted to accurately recall our experiences while working at AFSPPF. Actual dates of organizational establishments, etc. are presented in Chapter 1 of this document. George hand wrote the following summary and, out of respect for the significant role he played in our organization, it was transcribed unedited, for inclusion in this document. He was a great friend and a major contributor to the organization.

"My name is George Myers. The following is written as a narrative of events as I witnessed them."

"This history of the AFSPPF starts back about 1966, as far as I can recall. The unit was then the 8th Air Force Recci-Tech at Westover Air Force Base. I was assigned to the office of operations analysis at Headquarters 8th Air Force. Part of our responsibilities was to keep abreast of scientific and technical advances for the commander 8th Air Force. There was a program underway, called SAMOS, to develop launch vehicles to put satellites into orbit for military reasons. The program had been beset with many failures in the launch phase. It was known, at the time, that satellites were being developed for photoreconnaissance and that the resulting photography would be returned to Earth and would be processed at some secret location.

Suddenly, all memos and reports about SAMOS disappeared from normal technical and military channels.

The next development was that Eighth Air Force was requested to relinquish 8th Recci-Tech, for some reason. 8th Air Force tried to buck the request and was told to stop delaying the action. Of course, it turned out that the 8th Recci-Tech was to become Air Force Special Projects and work began to create a very large film processing facility. Apparently, at that time, the facility (6594th) was processing U-2 photography and beginning to handle the Corona project. Rumor had it that Col. Harold Ohlmeyer, commander 6594th; personally, hand carried the first photos of the Cuban Missile Crisis to the White House (This could not be verified). I digress here for a reason, which will become apparent later. 8th Air Force was firmly established at Westover Air Force Base. The base enjoyed good annual weather and was one of the bases nearest the European theater of operations; had a two-mile runway and could support B-52, U-2 and SR-71 operations. Of further major importance, was the three-level hardened underground command post, which was located under the Mount Holyoke mountain range. This command post was one of three national command sites built for at least $50 million. It was designated as the third level command post after one in Virginia serving the White House and the Pentagon, and the second at SAC Headquarters in Omaha, Nebraska. During the Cuban Missile Crisis, this 8th Air Force command post was manned and operational 24 hours a day for 30 days. Up to 25 B-52 aircraft were on airborne alert for the duration of the missile crisis. The existence of these command facilities and Westover Air Force Base were key factors in locating the processing facility for SAMOS, Corona and the programs, which followed.

Col. Ohlmeyer and Col. Fred Brown proceeded to build and equip a major processing facility capable of handling the processing of original satellite photography and printing the large number of duplicates required by the NRO. The facility was built to be the largest clean room processing and printing laboratory ever conceived. Col. Ohlmeyer was given carte blanche authority to build and equip and untold funding, to support its mission. The Trenton original processing machines and the Dalton duplication processing machines were built and installed with all the required supporting chemical and film handling systems and facilities. Of note was the fact that each system, which was built and installed at Westover Air Force Base, was also duplicated at Eastman Kodak. Key to the system design and installation was that everything was to be contained within a clean room atmosphere. This was the first major clean room ever constructed. Much work and engineering was done in an effort to reach a cleanliness level of 1.0 μ (Microns). That is, all particulate material larger than 1.0 μ was to be eliminated. It was found that this level of purity could be reached under quiet conditions but could not be held after many hours of operations. Therefore, all personnel entering and working in the laboratory were required to "suit up" with coveralls, headgear and booties before entering. The laboratory was maintained under a positive pressure and had air showers installed for entry and egress. When full operation began, Col. Ohlmeyer asked for and received the designation of Air Force Special Projects Production Facility (AFSPPF) for the unit and laboratory. Col. Ralph Swofford became the deputy commander of AFSPPF at about this time.

The R&D Directorate worked closely with Eastman Kodak and the Rochester Institute of Technology, both in Rochester, New York, to develop and finalize standards for mass production of photography. A standard was established for densitometric measurement of satellite imagery. Henceforth all measurements of density were made using a .5 mm aperture. Measurements were then a true reflection of the imagery on film. Processing standards were established with a duplication gamma of 1.0, a minimum density of .5 and a maximum density of 1.8. These standards were the criteria for accepting or rejecting mass-produced photography.

To aid the establishment of rigid controls over the printing and processing of photography in the laboratory, AFSPPF created a photographic standards laboratory to train technicians and maintain scientific control of the duplication process, from start to finish. Quality control was maintained by continuously sampling the sensitometry of the Dalton processors, the Niagara printing process and the densitometric readings in the laboratory. It must be noted that mass production of continuous imagery was required for various satellite camera systems in formats of (70 MM), 6, 9 and 12 inch widths.

AFSPPF developed a series of highly sophisticated light tables for the initial reading of frame-by-frame densities of the original photography and all resulting duplicates. These tables were motorized to handle roles of hundreds of feet of film, of the various sizes. Proper light sources were developed and densitometers were mounted to cover all fields of view.

AFSPPF worked with IBM on the adaption of the new IBM 1800 timeshare computer for automation of the laboratory. This computer continuously measured a large number of variables by sampling each variable over a short period. The 1800 computer was installed in the laboratory and monitored temperatures, chemistry, sensitometry, position of each roll of film in production and acceptance and rejection rates. This was probably the first use of a process control computer in a photographic production environment.

Col. Ohlmeyer had established and equipped a first-class photographic production facility. Col. Swofford decided the laboratory had to become as self-sufficient as possible. A diesel driven power plant was installed to ensure continuous electrical power. Three deep wells were drilled on Westover Air Force Base and a large water supply tank was built to avoid dissipation of the base water systems when AFSPPF was involved in continuous 24/7 production. Due to the enormous amount of chemicals, water and film used by the facility, pollution was beginning to be a problem. AFSPPF pioneered pollution control by establishing a facility to treat all waste materials generated by the laboratory and avoid any embarrassment to Westover Air Force Base.

During this period, silver had become a somewhat scarce commodity. AFSPPF conducted many studies with contractors to develop a non-silver film system. Several systems were developed, notably a Transparent Electro Photographic system (TEP), by James River Graphics Corporation. Silver recovery was a constant goal of the laboratory. These problems, and the major problem of dispersal of all the photographic film being generated by the NRO, were eased by the development, by AFSPPF, of a giant film shredder and incinerator. This system would take rolls of film as large as 12 inches in diameter, shred the film and spools and burn the residue. This system helped solve the problems of silver recovery and film disposal.

At one point in time, the intelligence community became involved with the possibility of color imagery from satellite systems. AFSPPF worked on this development for many years. A printer was developed with a full-color capability. The problem of developing film in full color at 100 ft/m was solved by the development of the Rainbow Processor. Unfortunately, the photo interpretation community did not consider imagery in full color to be near the quality and resolution of the black and white systems already in use. The need for color printing and processing vanished, after a few trials.

One benefit of the research done by AFSPPF was the improvement of the Niagara printer with a 1000-watt xenon light source. Superior printing at 100 ft/m, for films up to 12 inches in width, was assured by this development.

The primary mission of AFSPPF was to maintain the capability to develop satellite photography and produce sufficient duplicate reproductions, as required by the intelligence community. This required up to 30 duplicates of all photography recovered from satellite photographic systems in widths from (70mm) and 5 inches to 12 inches. At times, this mission required as many as 30 days of 24/7 operations.

AFSPPF was involved in many other facets supporting the NRO. From its very beginning, the facility conducted the CORN program for testing satellite systems. This involved sending crews out to lay down targets, which could be photographed by satellite cameras. The targets had to consist of bar resolution targets, of the proper size, to measure ground resolutions of the satellite. Gray scales were included to measure photographic density performance. Edge targets, meaning a sharp change of density, were used to derive ground resolution and hence the true photographic performance of the satellite. These targets covered several acres of ground and had to be laid in the precise location required by the satellites orbits. Many humorous stories were told about farmer's reactions to being requested to host CORN target layout.

The CORN program was one major part of satellite evaluation studies conducted by NRO teams working with the Evaluation Directorate at AFSPPF. Members of the Performance Evaluation Team (PET), including representatives from the National Photographic Intelligence Center (NPIC), the CIA, the NRO, DIA and SAMSO would gather at Westover Air Force Base, after each satellite mission. The team would spend days or weeks working on first duplicates and even the original negatives, in certain cases, on every mission, in order to ascertain satellite performance. They measured ground resolution, CORN target resolution, image quality and photographic performance as well as target coverage, weather and other orbital performance factors. Measuring ground resolution gave a measure of camera performance and the results of camera improvements and innovations. AFSPPF not only provided skilled evaluators for this work but also developed and improved machines called microdensitometers used to measure edge performance and hence ground resolutions. Contractors of AFSPPF worked continuously on programs for edge analysis to derive ground resolution.

AFSPPF was instrumental in convincing the intelligence community (NRO CIA NPIC etc.) that more emphasis needed to be given to the handling, processing and duplication of the received satellite photography. Hundreds of millions of dollars were spent producing the launch vehicles, satellite cameras, and orbital control and recovery systems. An enormous sum was being spent regularly by the intelligence community deriving the intelligence and measurements from the resulting duplicate photography. However, very little, figuratively, was being spent on the processing, printing and preparation of the duplicates, which was AFSPPF's mission.

When the intelligence community realized that this was the true state of the state-of-the-art, more attention was paid to the film production phase of the satellite film delivery system. One major development, resulting from this study, was a photographic imaging evaluation system using Photo Interpreters (P.I.'s) as evaluators. It was found that many factors, other than ground resolution, affected photographic quality. Every succeeding mission was evaluated from a P.I. point of view. Major advances were made to improve image performance including viscous processing, an improved duplication film (S0190) and improve image evaluation.

AFSPPF was involved with the Change Configuration Board (CCB) from the very beginning. Quarterly meetings were held, successively, at EK, SAMSO, CIA and AFSPPF. Proposals were made to the CCB, where they were approved and funded or disapproved, mainly to do with R&D projects. The CCB organized and hosted meetings with leading optical, camera and image analysis experts, usually held at AFSPPF.

As discussed earlier, Westover Air Force Base was considered a big base in long-range planning by the air staff and DOD. 8th Air Force was informed that, because of its location, base facilities in the closely hardened underground command post, Westover Air Force Base would continue to operate and Barksdale Air Force Base (2nd AF) would be closed. However, Sen. Ted Kennedy drove off the bridge at Chappaquiddick, Massachusetts and the political picture changed rapidly. Within 72 hours 8th Air Force was informed that plans were changed and Westover Air Force Base would no longer be an active base. 8th Air Force would be moved to Barksdale, Louisiana.

This changed the entire picture for AFSPPF. An operation of its size and complexity could no longer be kept from public view, with the base closing. Further complications had developed with the advent of the "T" (We believe this to be a reference to the TAGBOARD drone) program. Efforts were made to arrange for downloading facilities at AFSPPF, but this was deemed an impractical arrangement. Therefore, the NRO decided to close AFSPPF and move the duplication mission elsewhere. Effectively, AFSPPF closed in September 1976 (Actual date was December 31, 1976)."

George J. Myers,
Technical Director (Ret)
AFSPPF, Westover Air Force Base, Massachusetts

CHAPTER 10

Associated Military Organizations

497ᵗʰ RTG (Reconnaissance Technical Group)

The 497ᵗʰ RTG was activated in 1967 at Shierstein Kaserne, Wiesbaden, West Germany, as a covert imagery intelligence interpretation and reporting facility, just a few miles from the Wiesbaden Air Base. Subordinate units: 7113 Special Activities Squadron; 495ᵗʰ RTS; 496ᵗʰ RTS; Det. 1, 497ᵗʰ RTG.

The 497ᵗʰ RTG was a non-flying organization. Its mission included the processing, reproduction, and interpretation of aerial reconnaissance imagery, and preparation of intelligence reports. Also produced were tactical and strategic charts, mosaics and other types of target materials for cold war activities. The 497ᵗʰ RTG reported directly to the U.S. Commander In Chief, Europe, Allied Command, Europe, and certain USA intelligence agencies. Joint imagery exploitation expertise was provided by Army, Navy, and Air Force officers, technicians, and analysts. Special precision laboratory technical assistance was often provided by former AFSPPF personnel stationed at the Wiesbaden AB facility.

Prior to 1967, the 497ᵗʰ RTG was known as the 497ᵗʰ RTS (Reconnaissance Technical Squadron), which was established and activated in 1951 to accomplish, essentially, the same mission. The 497ᵗʰ RTS was expanded and became re-designated 497ᵗʰ RTG in 1967. The 497ᵗʰ RTS was billeted at the Lindsey Air Station in Wiesbaden, West Germany, but was actually located in the Shierstein Kaserne, near the Rhine River.

Rhine River Patrol: A taste of the real life

An interesting story is hereby told by former TSgt Erich Kassler. Erich served in the 497ᵗʰ RTS in the early days and is a member of our group. It is hoped that this will give the reader an idea of what life was like back then, when it was time to play.

"While stationed overseas I was assigned to the USAF 497ᵗʰ RTS, in Wiesbaden Germany. We were billeted at Lindsey Air Station and worked, in a secure compound, in the small town of Schierstein, along the Rhine River. This compound served as a Gestapo type hospital in WW2, which was evident because of the big Red Cross still visible on the roof of the main building. Torture leg and arm chains were still in place in the Sub-Subbasement. Yes, there was a Sub-Subbasement.

Our unit had a club in Schierstein Harbor, which we called the Yacht Club. We had no yachts but did lots of drinking there. It was a membership only club but we gave free access to the Navy personnel in the Rhine River Patrol unit, stationed at the harbor. This was a win-win situation for all of us. The Navy guys got to partake in our drinking facilities and we got access to the Navy Ship Store where we could get a carton of cigarettes for $1 (10 cents per pack) and a bottle of Cognac for .89 cents, with our script. At that time, we did not use USA Dollars but a paper script in denominations of 5, 10, 25, 50 Cents and 1, 5, and 10 Dollar values. Cigarettes, although rationed, were the common barter item on the German Black Market. Not legal but almost everyone used them as such. The German's didn't really like US cigarettes, as they were stronger than their own, but, in the long run, were actually cheaper for them to buy at $5 per carton. The only other thing I remember being more useful was Rock & Roll and Everly Brothers records from stateside. These were the favorites of the girls.

Gasoline was only 10 cents per gallon at a GI pump and about $5 per gallon at a German Station. Due to this fact, gas was more closely controlled. It was kept off the Black Market by the imposition of higher penalties, if you were caught selling it. It turns out, not many Germans could afford a car or gas until they were about 30 years old. The bicycle was the transportation mode of choice and necessity, for most. The Germans had an attitude about Americans, during this time. They used to say Americans were overpaid, over sexed and over there.

In 1958, the Rhine River Patrol was disbanded in Schierstein and the facilities returned to German control. We helped the Navy guys clean out their buildings and scrounged up all the big 5-gallon galvanized buckets we could. What do you do with all those 5-gallon buckets? Well, we took them back to our "Yacht Club" and filled them all with beer.

Shortly thereafter, one of the Navy guys "Borrowed" a patrol boat and we went for a pleasure cruise on the Rhine River to celebrate the Base closure. Of course, the 5-gallon buckets, full of beer, came with us. If you have ever drank beer out of a galvanized bucket you probably know what the end result was. Yep, we all got sick, very sick and very drunk. To make matters worse and more embarrassing, we ran out of gas on the river and had to be towed back to the harbor by a private German yacht. The yacht owner was a pretty nice guy and took pity on us. After all, I guess it gave him a story to tell, as well. Bottom line, we got through it in one piece and learned a few good lessons in the process. At least we can't say it was all work and no play."

See related photos below.

Military Script

Wiesbaden Yacht Club

497th & Rhine River Patrol

Yacht Club

Erich Kassler 1958

USAF 497th RTS/USN Rhine River Patrol, in Wiesbaden Germany (Photos by Erich Kassler)

7499th SG (Support Group)

The 7499th SG was activated in 1955 and located at Wiesbaden AB, West Germany. It consisted of three subordinate flying squadrons: 7405th, 7406th and the 7407th Support Squadrons. It was inactivated in 1974 and combined with the 497th RTS (Reconnaissance Technical Squadron) at Schierstein Kaserne, Wiesbaden, West Germany.

The 7499th SG participated in overt and covert intelligence collection activities during the Cold War. Reconnaissance coverage included the Berlin, Germany Air Corridors where courier cargo/passenger aircraft were used as a cover, but were armed with covertly hidden aerial cameras. During the Cold War, the 7405th Support Squadron and sister flying squadrons increasingly flew peripheral top-secret reconnaissance missions throughout Europe and the Middle East.

The 7499th SG assets included a 24/7 intelligence precision processing laboratory, discretely located, with approximately 60 photo technicians working under clean room conditions and with state-of the-art imagery processing, reproduction, and quality control equipment. This photo lab was the central processing center for all low and high altitude USAF/DOD directed aerial reconnaissance and intelligence collection programs in Europe. In 1972, SR-71 support was added to the lab's processing support requirements.

Most equipment procurements and personnel manning requirements were secretly sponsored and/or coordinated by the AFSPPF. Equipment assets came from surplus assets at the AFSPPF, or from discretely authorized manufacturers in the USA. "Black" operating accounts were used to maintain security and bypass the typical USAF logistics systems.

Aerial reconnaissance imagery, processed and produced by this laboratory, was delivered by armed courier to the 497th RTG at Schierstein Kaserne.

Top Secret messages for the 7499th SG always arrived at the 497th RTG and were safely stored in their secured vault. The processing facility at Wiesbaden AB, in the early years, did not have a suitable vault for permanent storage of Top Secret documents. Cleared personnel commuted between the two facilities to access these classified messages, as required.

67th RTS (Reconnaissance Technical Squadron)

Activated at Yokota AB, Japan, July 1957, as a subordinate squadron of the 67th Reconnaissance Technical Wing, also located at Yokota AB.

Inactivated in 1971, whereby certain assets and personnel phased into the 548th Reconnaissance Technical Group at Hickam AFB, HI.

The 67th RTS was a discrete covert central imagery processing, reproduction, and intelligence exploitation center for Cold War intelligence activities in Asia. It was a non-flying unit, reporting to 5th Air Force, and operated with approximately 350 assigned personnel.

The AFSPPF primarily used the 67th RTS as a reliable source of highly trained personnel with security clearances. Upon completion of tour assignments, selected personnel were assigned to the AFSPPF. The 67th RTS did not rely upon the AFSPPF for technical and equipment procurement assistance as much as the USAFE and DOD units did in Europe. The 67th RTS supported many different high altitude airborne platforms including the U-2, A-12 and SR-71.

Procurement of specialized equipment and supplies was accomplished with the help of certain USA based intelligence agencies, in addition to authorized commercial enterprises. This was done through secret channels. "Black" accounts were used to bypass normal USAF logistics channels. The 67th RTS mission included the production of charts, mosaics, and other types of target materials for tactical and strategic use in PACAF war plans and for other cold war interests in Asia. In order to accomplish this variety of work, discrete intelligence agencies in the USA provided certain "sanitized" satellite KH-series intelligence imagery to assist in meeting these production requirements.

The large "H" shaped building, 206, and immediately surrounding buildings, was home of the 67th Reconnaissance Technical Squadron, Yokota AB, Japan. Circa 1957-1971 (US Air Force Photo by Mark Nelson)

6594th TG (Test Group) / 6593rd TS (Test Squadron)

The 6594th TG / 6593rd TS were stationed at Hickam AFB, Hawaii. Their primary mission was to intercept and recover the film buckets dropped from our reconnaissance satellites and deliver them to the CONUS for processing. They used modified cargo planes; namely C-119 Flying Boxcars and later, C-130 Hercules, to snatch the film buckets from mid-air, as they floated down under parachutes. The first successful mid-air recovery was in mid August 1960 when a C-119 Boxcar recovered a film bucket from a Corona mission. This was the first successful recovery of film from an orbiting satellite and the first aerial recovery of an object returning from Earth orbit. This was the only organization to serve in this capacity throughout the entire Film Return Satellite program.

The following photo shows an original C-119 Boxcar doing its job:

C-119 Flying Boxcar – Initial Film Bucket Recovery Vehicle
(US Air Force Photo)

The following three photos show the Bucket recovery sequence with a JC-130B aircraft.

JC-130B coming for a Bucket
(US Air Force Photo)

JC-130B about to snatch a Bucket
(US Air Force Photo)

JC-130B Bucket snatched and in tow
(US Air Force Photo)

8th RTS (Reconnaissance Technical Squadron)

As mentioned in Chapter 1, the 8th RTS occupied building P1900 from the beginning and was co-located with AFSPPL during the early 1960's. Primary mission of the 8th RTS was Cartography (map making) for SAC (Strategic Air Command). Bombing maps were made by designating targets within cities, towns or wherever. Information came from aircraft and satellite photos and other known facts. This information was then scribed onto scribe coat and subsequently printed onto maps, accentuating roads, streams, terrain, buildings, etc. and accurately pinpointing bombing targets. Revisions of older maps were made from updated satellite and aerial photos. Pertinent data was added to the maps and unnecessary data was eliminated, to reduce clutter and allow the user to more clearly see the targets. This process of Cartography can also be simply defined as the science of enhancing an image or map to help the user accomplish their mission by adding notations or special symbols to designate unique features to quickly point the user to an objective or destination.

Several key people, from the organization, were transferred to AFSPPL. This formed the basis of the AFSPPL organization, in the beginning. In the later years, AFSPPF supplied the 8th RTS with satellite photography, as required, to assist them in their mission. It is doubtful they ever knew where the photos came from, even though they were almost next door. This was the nature of security back then. It was rumored they played a role in the Cuban Missile Crisis; however the facts are it was AFSPPL. Westover AFB records are incorrect, on this matter. The confusion is understandable, since both organizations were collocated in the same building, during the Cuban Missile Crisis period, and AFSPPL personnel records were not located on base, as mentioned in Chapter 1. Base personnel had no idea what was going on in building P1900.

Today, several of their members have joined the AFSPPF reunion ranks. In fact, one of their members, Richard (Dick) Temple, has been our reunion coordinator for the past several years and has done a superb job. Thanks to Dick's efforts, we're not only getting to know more about our respective organizations, but we are having a great time, in the process. We are renewing old friendships and making many new ones, as well. It should be noted, that we have no corporate sponsorship. Every member of our reunion has paid his or her own way to each and every reunion event, thus far.

Dick Temple arrived at Westover AFB in November 1967, whereby he was assigned to the 8th RTS. Following is a summary of his story:

He was officially called a Photometric Cartographic Analysis Technician, but simply known as a Cartographer. Because of his performance, he was asked if he wanted to work in the Special Projects section of the unit. Of course, he said yes. He recalls that to enter the Special Projects section, one had to trade their yellow badge for a red badge. The guard would then "buzz" you into his small area where you would proceed down some steps and go to a door, located behind a curtain. The curtain was there to insure that no one could see you enter a set of numbers into a cipher key pad, whose pass code numbers were changed each month. Once inside, it seemed like you were entering a basement but it was a place where "special people worked on special projects". The space was obviously below ground, as it had a very low ceiling and did not extend the whole length of the building above. It also contained a smaller, inside vault, which was used to store "extra special items". Classified material could be left out overnight, in the general working space, but certain items had to be returned to the inside vault, at the end of each day. This was his working environment for several years. Although smaller in area, this working environment was very similar to that of the AFSPPF, regarding badge exchanges, cipher locks, vaulted rooms, etc.

Two memorable moments were recalled about his assignment there. The first was not being selected as Airman of the Quarter and the second was beating the AFSPPF softball team for the 1969 base championship (a rare event). Regarding the first recalled moment, he was one of three people nominated but, as the selection day approached, he found out later, one of the candidates didn't qualify and another had been transferred. That left only him and, since there was only one candidate left, the selection team decided to not pick anyone for that quarter. So, in other words, he competed for Airman of the Quarter against himself and lost. How humiliating!

On March 31, 1970, the Eighth Air Force, including the 8th RTS, was deactivated and he received orders to go to the 2nd RTS in Barksdale AFB, Shreveport, LA. Not having quite completed his four-year enlistment, he was not eligible to receive a re-up bonus and, since the division officer would not try to obtain a waiver to receive it, he decided to leave the Air Force. He, subsequently joined the Navy (what was he thinking?) and became a carrier fighter pilot (a slightly riskier job, but not bad). We are now happy he has become a member of our group and once again joined the Air Force.

CHAPTER 11

Special Stories of Accomplishments and Interesting Incidents

The following stories were submitted by Lt Col, USAF Ret. Samuel (Sam) D. McCulloch, who was assigned to our facility in the formative years, from Jan 1962 to Dec 1965.

EVALUATE THIS! "PET" IS BORNE

"In the very early days, we were assigned the job of developing and implementing an image evaluation program. As photo interpreters, the guys knew a bit about image quality and I maybe knew somewhat more as the result of my Photo School training and my experience in the 2nd RTS Photo lab, but not much more. Therefore, we began by developing a set of characteristics that we felt needed to be assessed on the imagery and then proceeded to develop a set of procedures we could use to measure those characteristics. We did not do this without considerable help from others in the R&D Directorate but especially from numerous specialists, mostly from various companies and one individual, a professor from the Rochester Institute of Technology, Dr. Shoemaker. Among the several companies that assisted in developing the evaluation procedures were Eastman Kodak, Perkin-Elmer and especially the Data Corporation. We were later identified as the Performance Evaluation Team (PET).

There were about ten characteristics used to evaluate imagery. One of which was the degree of "resolution" (sharpness, clarity) of the details seen in the images. One of the individuals assigned to Evaluation was MSgt

Joe Franklin. One of Joe's earlier assignments was working with the U-2 pilots at their home base at which he evaluated the image quality from their training missions in terms of image motion, so corrections could be made by whatever means. Joe used a technique developed by the Hycon Corporation (who built the camera system) called "edge spread" measured in fractions of an inch or of a millimeter. Therefore, we began to apply that technique, as one of the means for assessing image quality, calling it "Reciprocal Edge Spread", so it would be similar in format to resolution historically measured from special resolution targets. The specialists who advised us from time to time were quite disturbed by the simplicity of the method and certainly questioned its validity, and there were numerous meetings of groups and individuals to discuss the technique. I had the dubious honor of making a presentation to one such group in which I explained the technique. Nevertheless, as we began working with a team of individuals from the office responsible for developing the new satellite reconnaissance programs, we found that they were quite satisfied with our results, and at least one program that I recall us assisting them on, eventually became operational.

The results of our image evaluations were used to prepare a report on each mission that was then used by the system program managers to prepare their report on the mission. Captain Herb Duval later assisted in preparation of the reports we issued, with the typing done by a civilian, Liz Dostal. Herb later became the Director of the Evaluation Directorate after it was formally organized. Another individual instrumental in preparation of these reports was Charlie Rauscher, a civilian, who managed the Graphics Division and was a major reason for the success of the reports. Others in the group, at this time, were SSgt Joe Kubacki, SSgt Jack Strobel, and CMSgt Bill Kuyper. Capt. John Hilton was the computer guru who provided the automated support we needed to analyze and document some of the results of the evaluations. I met frequently with Lt Col Williams about the status of the evaluation effort on each mission and, on occasion, I visited Washington D.C. with him to attend technical meetings."

ROCKS

"One of my tasks, during the operation of the reconnaissance mission, was to guide a team from Data Corp to huge resolution targets on the ground, usually on USAF bases, such that the team would be situated along the planned track of the satellite. I was in contact with both the system folks and the team on the ground that had to drive to the location of the ground resolution targets and be in place at the appropriate time so they could collect various environmental data at the time the images were being recorded. Ordinarily, the team had plenty of time to get to the ground target. On one occasion, however, the track was changed at the last minute. I, therefore, contacted Data Corp (in the days prior to cell phones) and they sent a small plane with a note tied on a rock. They found the vehicle, with the team on board travelling down the highway, and dropped the rock (with note attached). Somehow, it worked, no one got hurt and the team subsequently turned and went to the new location, in time to gather the appropriate data at the appointed time. They dropped a rock! You have to be kidding. This is the true definition of getting the job done and thinking outside the box."

LOST FOREVER

"There was one special project when the group actually served as Photo Interpreters (PIs). A reconnaissance satellite had gone down and was thought to be somewhere in North America. Therefore, a series of U-2 missions were flown in attempt to find and, I suppose, recover the downed satellite, if possible. While the guys reviewed the film, I was in contact with the U-2 office to tell them where cloud cover occurred so that the cloud-covered area could be flown over again. They did not find the downed satellite, which we learned later probably went down in the Indian Ocean. So in terms of accomplishments, the idea of converting a group of image interpreters, who typically looked for military targets on images, and then documented what they saw, into a group of image evaluation technicians, whose results were acceptable, was nothing short of phenomenal."

U-2 SUPPORT

"Regarding my third task, as executive secretary to Col. Ohlmeyer's committee, I was especially interested in the project to establish OPIC-A because it was to be that part of the 67th RTS at Yokota in which we had conducted the U-2 missions not long before my assignment to AFSPPF. In addition, the CIA representative to the Committee had been one of the two who directed our work on the missions while I was in the 67th RTS. Thanks to Col. Ohlmeyer's patience and that of the committee members, the facility was established, as described in the history of the 67th RTS prepared by Lt Col Roy Stanley."

TOP BRASS CHAUFFER

"One kind of embarrassing memory, and yet one that was of great benefit to me, occurred as the result of Col. Ohlmeyer and I taking trips to the Pentagon, for the Committee he chaired. The first time we flew to Washington, D.C., we discussed the driving situation, once we got there. I said that I would of course do the driving to and from the airport and the Pentagon but noted that I did not know anything about the D.C. area. Col. Ohlmeyer immediately said that he knew the area well and would do the driving. As a result, during all the trips we took for the Committee meetings, he did the driving, with me a brand new Captain. I doubt that he ever understood how much I appreciated his doing that for me. Maybe he was concerned about his personal safety with me driving in a strange town, but I don't think so. During our visits to the NRO office, Col. Ohlmeyer introduced me to the Director of the NRO staff, BG James Stewart, and the then DNRO, Dr. Joseph V. Charyk."

TRAVEL PROBLEMS

"I inadvertently helped set a precedent for one specific type of activity. Since our parent unit (the NRO) was located in the Pentagon, several members of the unit made frequent trips to that office. As a junior Captain, I probably was asked to go about as often as anyone did, and usually carried a gun in a shoulder holster because I was usually carrying classified materials to and from the NRO office. I usually travelled alone with a relatively small amount of cash and had maybe one gas credit card at the time. I would park my car at the Hartford-Springfield Airport, fly to Washington National Airport, take a taxi to the Pentagon, conduct my business, take a taxi back to the Airport, and fly back to my car and then on to the base, with no difficulties. There was one trip, however, that stands out in my memory.

On one of these trips, when the weather was exceptionally bad, the flight back to the base departed from the usual schedule and I was dumped in Philadelphia, Pa. I had enough cash to purchase a bus ticket as far as Hartford, CT, with a good distance from there to my car. En route, I had one change of buses in far West New York City, where I waited for the next bus outside. I was carrying a large leather-strapped briefcase that had a lock and contained classified material, a .38 revolver strapped to my shoulder, under a cheap Italian silk suit I had bought in Japan, the bullets in my pocket as required by Security, and growing gray hair as I waited. I then got the bus on to Hartford. When I stepped off the bus, into knee-deep snow about midnight or so, I had two dimes on my person. I could not afford a hotel, but would not have been able to sleep anyway with the classified material I carried, so I walked into an overnight restaurant and ordered a cup of coffee for a dime. Then with my last dime, I called Ken Saylor to discuss the situation. He asked that I just stay put and he and SSgt Donald Hoar, his assistant in Security, would come for me. They did so and took me to get my car. I followed them back to the base with, by then, the roads being cleared somewhat by the road crews. They took the classified material to the office and I went home to a worried wife. The result was that, from that time on, it was required that anyone carrying classified materials would have sufficient cash on hand and would travel in pairs."

COMMERCIAL AIR FUN

"The following incident occurred on a subsequent trip. This time I had sufficient funds for emergencies. I was accompanied by SSgt Joe Kubacki, a photo interpreter on the PET staff. The procedure for checking into the airport terminal was to inform the check-in desk that I was an armed military courier and would release the weapon to the aircraft pilot if requested, which never occurred. We were further advised that, in the event we arrived too late to visit the normal check-in counter, I should go straight to the appropriate gate and, as I boarded the plane, I was to inform a stewardess that I was an armed military courier and would release the weapon to the pilot if requested to do so. As luck would have it, we were late leaving the NRO office, took a taxi to the airport, went straight to the boarding gate, and walked out to the aircraft. A stewardess met us as we walked up the stairs and I told her that I was an armed military courier and would turn the weapon over to the pilot for the duration of the flight if requested. The stewardess was of course surprised but told us to proceed with boarding. I took a seat and Joe sat about two rows behind me. Early in the flight, I saw the stewardess I had spoken to coming down the aisle and she was whispering loudly to another stewardess and pointing to me saying, "That guy is armed". Joe heard the comment, as well, and quickly pulled the newspaper he was reading up high in an attempt to hide. I had no idea what would happen next but noted they were watching me closely each time they walked down the aisle to deliver coffee or whatever. The remainder of the flight was uneventful but I am sure the flight staff was relieved when we left the plane. I believe Joe was even more relieved than they were. I reported the incident to Ken Saylor so future couriers would be aware of the possible situations they might encounter. I strongly suspect this type of incident would never happen in today's environment."

SPECIAL DUTY

"During one of my trips to the NRO office, Major Lescotti showed me an oblique aerial enlargement of a facility somewhere in New Mexico. He asked that I memorize the image, as I was not allowed to take a copy with me, and henceforth I would be sent, periodically, rolls of film taken by the X-15 aircraft during experimental flights out of, I think, Edwards AFB. On occasion, the aircraft might roll over such that this facility could be shown on one or more frames of the film. In those cases I was to cut the frames showing that facility from the roll, splice the roll back together, prepare an evaluation of the quality of the film on the roll, send the roll back to the source and get the extracted frames and the report to the NRO office or to the National Photographic Interpretation Center (NPIC). I subsequently asked that one other person be assigned to assist me in the project or to handle it in my absence.

TSgt Ed Comer was asked to participate in the project. I do not recall if Ed was later able to see the original photo or if I just described the facility to him. In any event, we worked together on several rolls of film, over time, and became good friends. We had a great time reviewing the film and had some great laughs over how to describe some of the image quality aspects (e.g., how to describe a squashed bug in one case). At some point Ed had applied for a commission as a Warrant Officer in the U.S. Army and subsequently received the appointment. He asked me to conduct the ceremony to swear him in, which I did. Afterwards we went to the Officer's Club for a brief celebration. We have maintained contact all these years."

POLITICS – Wife to the Rescue

"One memory, which involved a bit of politics, began in part with a series of minor problems I was having at the outset of my assignment to AFSPPF. The initial assignment of the photo interpreters in the unit was apparently not well publicized. In fact, I had one minor encounter in that regard shortly after I arrived. The PI group agreed that we could each make good use of a Photo Interpretation (PI) Kit, a standard issue in most assignments where photo interpretation was done. Therefore, I approached Capt. Frank Curtis, Director of the Logistics and Supply Directorate, and told him of our request. I was told, in no uncertain terms, that a photo lab had no authorization for issuance of PI Kits. I told Frank that might be true but we were in a separate unit from the lab and could use these kits, since we were in fact Photo Interpreters (PI's). Frank was skeptical but agreed to research the files and let me know the outcome.

At the same time, I was having some difficulty with Capt. Ken Saylor, head of Security, about some matter I do not recall, and had hit a snag in whatever I had requested. There was a third problem; however, I cannot remember it. Anyway, I mentioned to my wife that I was having some minor difficulties getting support from several of the offices headed up by Captains. So my wife, Anita, decided to see if she could help solve the problem by hosting a party that included these and other folks of similar rank.

We lived on base in a limited space so she decided to limit the attendance by sending out invitations that referenced the party as being for Company Grade officers. We had hopes that, if anyone showed up at all, the weather would accommodate us and allow the party to be held outdoors. It did not cooperate and, in fact, every single Company Grade officer and their wives or girl friends showed up, so we held the party indoors in a cramped space. Each family brought their own drinks and snacks and we danced in the small living room, and had a great time.

Within a few days, Frank came to me and said he had just ordered 15 of the kits because the organization did indeed have PIs assigned. The problem I had with Ken also was resolved immediately. Later on, one of the individuals attending the party commented to me that he and others had thought it was a mandatory organization party by our noting it was for Company Grade officers.

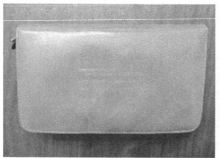 

P.I. Kit in Case   P.I. kit
(Photo by Lloyd R. Spanberger)   (Photo by Lloyd R. Spanberger)

The result was that we had continuing parties once a month at someone's house or at the officer's club from then on and the relationship between the officers in the unit was great. Not too long after these social gatherings began, I was approached by one of the Field Grade officers, a Major in the organization, asking if he and his wife could be invited to some of the parties. From that time on, he and all of the officers were invited and many of the Field Grade folks became part of the group on a continuing basis, including Col. Brown.

The social events that brought so many of us together aided immensely in our ability to work together at AFSPPF. Captain Lou Falconieri and his wife LaVonne have been friends since then and Lou and I subsequently worked together in Texas State government for a time. Frank and Janet Curtis were among our best friends. We later lived near them in the D.C. area, during my last year in service, and I continue to be in touch with Janet."

The following stories relate to the author, former AF Captain and Research Physicist, Lloyd Spanberger, who was assigned to the facility in the R&D Directorate from 1966 to 1968.

LOST IN DC

It was sometime in mid September 1967. This was my first trip to the NPIC in Washington DC and I was looking forward to it with enthusiasm. I had been working with several members of the NPIC staff and they had been to our facility many times to discuss various aspects of image analysis, film-processing techniques, etc. One particular cause of disagreement was the constant use of photographic terminology, that wasn't conducive to scientific analysis and ease of calculations. Terms like Lumens and Candlepower, for example. These terms are not easily used in equations related to energy and power calculations. My goal was to get the community to change to standard terminology, such as, Joules (Energy) and Watts (Power), etc. What could be simpler? There were other terms to be considered, as well. However, it was the concept I was interested in. It was an attempt to bring the science of photography out of the Black Magic Photo world into the real world of science and technology, where one could use real equations to figure things out.

It seemed to me that many contractor personnel were doing their best to keep confusion in the game and wanted to hang on to the old, so-called, photo terms. I believe it's still a problem to this day. We were also scheduled to discuss other technical matters, such as low gamma and dual gamma processing, alternate film types (such as Non-silver), the merits of the Tri Bar and other CORN targets, etc. You know; all that boring technical stuff.

It was to be a multi day trip and I had a motel confirmed nearby the NPIC facility and a rental car reserved. All was good. Turns out, however, it was my first trip to NPIC and I wasn't all that used to the DC area, although I had been to the Pentagon in the past. NPIC was located in the

US Navy Yard, Washington DC, which, unfortunately, was across the river from National Airport. After spending a full day at work, I hopped a plane to DC from the Springfield/Hartford Airport. If I recall correctly, my wife, Mary, drove me to the airport and promised to pick me up upon my return. There was no time for dinner, but I think I got a small bag of peanuts or something on the plane. I figured I would have time for a light dinner when I got to the motel. Little did I know of the adventure about to happen!

I arrived in DC late at night, got my car and off I went to the motel. Well, wouldn't you know, it wasn't there. It only took me well over an hour or so, in DC traffic, to get there and now, it didn't exist. Here I thought I was the one who didn't exist. I was beginning to think no one existed. Of course, I could have used my GPS to find it, but wait; that hadn't been invented yet. Oh well, there were always those things called MAPS. Have you ever tried reading a DC map while driving a car at night? Ok I should have stopped and read it, but I was in a not so friendly neighborhood and was not about to stop. That's probably not politically correct today (you never know who you could offend anymore), but I don't care. It finally dawned on me that there was this quadrant system in DC and I was probably in the wrong one, without knowing it. Apparently, when I drove over the bridge, I took a wrong turn and that started the whole ordeal. I followed the street I thought I was supposed to be on, etc. and was getting nowhere. It got to be after 2 AM in the morning and I had had it. Where was a cell phone when you needed one? Why did I not just call the motel and ask for directions? Did I say ask directions? You have to be kidding! Guys just don't do that.

I was reading the James Bond novels, at this point in my life, and I got to thinking about what he would do in a situation like this. Well, guess what, Q did not show up with any special gadgets to get me out of trouble and no hot blond drove up in an exotic sports car to give me a ride to my destination (Probably a good thing, by the way). Desperation finally set in and I found a cop on duty. I pulled over next to him, did the unthinkable and asked how to get to the motel. He was very understanding and got me on track.

Good thing my reservation was guaranteed. I got something to eat from a vending machine and hit the sack. Although I was very tired the next day and took my share of ribbing, I had a great meeting with the NPIC people. This trip made me an almost expert on navigating DC (I have since lost that ability). The result was that the meetings went well and I got an excellent tour of the facility. In particular, I was very impressed with their model shop and top-secret library, where I had a chance to browse for about an hour between meetings. It was very informative and enlightening. Does the "kid in a candy store" concept ring any bells?

I learned that the model shop was used to construct scale models of Soviet and Red Chinese installations, right along with their actual construction. Apparently, among other things, these models were used to keep target keys up to date, should the military need to take out these installations. It was very cool to see these models first hand. The imagery our National Reconnaissance Program provided sure did help. Finding out what they were building was quite a revelation, to say the least. At any rate, they weren't getting away with it without being observed by the good guys.

I also had the opportunity to see the first Gambit images of the Soviet "Caspian Sea Monster". Obviously, it was located in the Caspian Sea. The NPIC people were quite impressed with finding this extremely large seaplane, which I later found out was never meant to fly, except just over the water to hide from RADAR and only to carry troops and supplies. At the time, however, it was quite the buzz at NPIC. Overall, it was a great trip. I learned a lot and I hope I contributed a lot.

SORRY SAM

As I recalled this incident, I can't help thinking about the problem Sam McCulloch ran into when he got stranded knee deep in snow in Hartford, CT with only twenty cents to his name. Sorry Sam, I may have been all alone, like you were, but I got lucky. At least I had a car and a few extra coins for my vending machine dinner that night, even if I was lost. For once, I was able to afford dinner on military Per Diem (How lucky can one get?). As I now look back, I am so thankful I didn't have to go through what you had to endure. My problems were small change (No pun intended) in comparison. Oh yes, by the way, at this point in our units development, the bullets were in our guns when we had to carry them. Fortunately, one wasn't needed on this trip.

SORRY, WRONG PASSWORD

There was one incident on a MINIBALL run, that made for an exciting night, if you can call it that. An NCO (I cannot recall his name after so many years) and I were pulling courier duty on that run and we landed at Wright Patterson AFB, late at night. There were many stops to be made that evening and I cannot recall which one, in sequence, this was, although I suspect it was the last one, since it was so late at night. What transpired, however, is an incident I vividly remember. We landed without incident and taxied to a remote location some distance from the main hangers, Shortly thereafter, a black van pulled up to receive their classified material. We opened the cargo doors, greeted the people in the van and asked for the proper password. Well, wouldn't you know, they didn't have it right. Great, now what do we do? I was no longer sure these were the right guys, and refused delivery. Of course, they were somewhat upset and started to argue about it. Bottom line, they were sent to obtain the proper password and IDs, before any material was going to be given them. Yea, I was a little nervous and had my hand on my gun, in my pocket, just in case. I was somewhat sure it was just an administrative foul up but they had an attitude problem and I developed one.

I can't remember exactly how I got to the flight operations area. Either the pilot called for a vehicle or I walked across the runway. I believe it was in April 1967 and I do remember it was still a bit cold outside. In either case, I left the gun with my NCO, who stayed with the material, and I went to work the problem. Fortunately, the flight operations snack bar was still open and had a telephone. Back then, once again, we had no cell phones, so communications during late hours was a serious problem. Resolution of the problem took several hours. I finally connected with our facility security officer and relayed the problem. He, in turn, wound up waking several high-level security personnel in the middle of the night, but rules were rules. I'm sure the people in the black van were working the same problem, but I really didn't care. I couldn't just sit there and wait until they figured out what to do. We were getting behind schedule and the material was very sensitive and needed the proper care and handling. Once the proper calls were made, I got a bite to eat and went back to the plane to relieve my NCO. He then took his break, as I waited for the black van to reappear. He was only gone for about 45 minutes or so and just after getting back, the van arrived with the proper password, the material was delivered and away we went.

The good news was we all needed a break anyway and got a bite to eat and a rest stop (Even the pilot and flight crew). Locating people in the middle of the night was no easy task and delayed the mission considerably, but it couldn't be avoided. Proper procedures were always maintained. Fortunately, this didn't happen very often and, after this incident, I'm sure it became a rare event. For some unknown reason, higher-ranking officers didn't like being rousted out in the middle of the night. They didn't seem to care that we weren't having any fun either and were up all night. Go figure!

(The following short story was told by SMSgt. Leroy (Moose) Miller, at the 2012 AFSPPF Reunion, in Branson, Missouri.)

WHAT'S HAPPENING IN NEW YORK?

"One summer evening, Col Ohlmeyer wanted another NCO, along with me, to go with him to a specific address in a small town in upper New York State. It was about a 3 to 4 hour drive. The address was a small store in the downtown section of this town and we were told to arrive there after dark. Once we arrived, the Col. opened the door and had us enter. We were handed a roll of color film and asked to develop it (Everything we needed was there). We did so, handed the film back, and went home. *Never did know what was on that film!*"

WIVES STORIES

Cheryl Johnson story

"It was the week before Doug and I got married. He had to take one of his secret flights and I was going to use his car to get on base to go to the Officers Club, to finish the arrangements for the reception. Doug came and picked me up early in the morning and we drove over to the flight line on base, since he was flying out on a MAT or MAC plane. He parked the car, and went and got on the plane. I was sitting there in my nightgown and robe, with no keys. The plane had started engines, and I thought I was stuck there. He wasn't due back for about 3 days and I had no idea what to do. All of a sudden, the plane door opened and Doug came back down the stairs to give me the keys. Thank goodness, I didn't have to walk home in my nightgown. Since he was so good to me, I went and picked him up on his return."

Lynn Colville story

"Having been admitted to the base hospital at 6:00 AM for the impending birth of our first child, Lee was by my side all day. On the following morning, it was imperative that he report for work so I was left alone and anxious. Why was it necessary for him to leave me? Because he had to remain in his building or be declared dead if caught by the APs. This was the "Day of Great Effort" (simulated war) at Westover Air Force Base. As it happened, Rose Sanner, wife of TSgt Russ Sanner, who was in AFSPPL, was the nurse on duty in maternity that day. She kept assuring me that Lee would be there soon. Now when Captain Curtis learned that I was in the hospital, he told Lee that he should be with me. Colonel Ohlmeyer, who was in charge of sterile badges for essential personnel to navigate the base without fear of being incarcerated, personally called Lee and told him to report to the orderly room where he was given a badge and ordered to keep it as long as necessary. He arrived at the hospital wearing the "sterile" badge (You have to be kidding. How could that be? I was laboring to have our first-born.) It turns out he made several trips back and forth that afternoon and was with me for the birth of our son. Thank you, Col Ohlmeyer, for sterilizing my husband, I think."

COLLECTING SATELLITE SENSOR CALIBRATION DATA

(The following story was told by CMSgt Jim Grimm during one of our reunions)

"On one occasion, I made an urgent Top Secret trip to a remote missile site at Minot AFB, North Dakota to collect illumination data, urgently needed to calibrate satellite sensors. I had to be at Minot AFB no later than 2000 hours, when a satellite was scheduled to pass over the base. Illumination data to be collected near missile sites, aircraft landing strips, fuel and bomb dumps, and aircraft hangars.

The Top Secret message directing the project was received by AFSPPF Security about 0800 hours of day one. At 1000 hours, with a special light meter in hand, I drove to Bradley Field, CT. and boarded a commercial aircraft to Denver, CO., where I transferred to a single engine aircraft and headed to Minot, ND, arriving about 1400 hours at a small airport in the middle of, what seemed like nowhere. Waiting for me was my escort (a Colonel), with an Air Force blue sedan, ready to whisk me away to the Base Commander's office.

The message required that direct logistical assistance had to be provided by the missile Base Commander, who did not have the appropriate security clearance. Administratively, in order to support me, the Commander was required to provide a high-level officer with appropriate transportation to and from the local airport, and to any place on Minot AFB where I wanted to go to conduct illumination measurements. The Colonel was also responsible for arranging for my subsistence while at Minot AFB. I'm sure he enjoyed every minute of his assignment.

The Base Commander explained to me that he had received an important message from the Department of the Air Force stating that I would be arriving to conduct an illumination project, and that I was to receive full support with no questions asked. I read the message before I departed the AFSPPF and was aware of the Commander's responsibilities. He was very inquisitive about where I was from and exactly what I was going to do. I politely told him it was a highly classified matter, he did not have a need to know, and that all he had to do was comply with the message. After that, he was probably satisfied that I wasn't going to blow up his Base and he finally stopped his interrogation. Here I am, a Chief Master Sergeant, telling an O-6 Base Commander his responsibility regarding the project. Of course, during my Air Force career, this wasn't the first time I used my position of authority to override somebody with higher rank! Fortunately, I learned how to handle these administrative problems early in my military career.

Collecting the illumination data went smooth; however, my driver Colonel kept trying to squeeze information out of me (probably so he could relay it to the Base Commander who was still curious about the project). The data collected that night, were classified and immediately forwarded to higher headquarters, via classified Air Force channels, upon my return to the AFSPPF. Although the information had to be collected in a timely manner, the results were not needed until the corresponding film was returned from the satellite, many days later.

Fortunately, my return trip to the AFSPPF was not urgent, because it took three miserable days. With my luck, the commercial airliner, I was flying on, landed at the wrong airport at about 2200 hours in New York, with no transportation available to move passengers to the correct airport. I slept on an airport hard bench that night until passengers could be moved to the correct airport the next day. The bottom line; my trip to Minot, ND took about six hours and my return trip took three days; another travel bummer."

FIRST MOON LANDING

(The following final tidbit is recalled from Capt. Blaine Thacker's memories.)

"One of the most memorable projects handled was the camera shots from the first moon landing in 1969. Our facility was tasked to make enhanced color duplicates on one of our advanced printers. This was done on an unclassified basis. As a result, a few AFSPPF personnel were privileged to keep the "official rejects" of those shots for themselves."

CHAPTER 12

Conclusion

It is hoped that this history of the AFSPPF will provide the reader with a thorough understanding of the mission of our facility during the early and subsequent stages of Film Return Satellite Reconnaissance, in this country, during the Cold War period. The cold war was won, in large part, due to the National Reconnaissance Program consisting of the many facets of reconnaissance. Satellites, spy aircraft and satellite and spy aircraft related organizations, all played a critical role in providing our military and political leaders with the intelligence needed to make the important decisions that made it possible. Our intelligence systems today are far superior to what we had back then and we can only hope our leaders of today have the foresight to use them, and the data they collect, properly and effectively.

As mentioned previously, we were but a small part of the big picture; but did our job and provided the best possible product to our intelligence community, at that time. Although, in the grand scheme of things, we were a relatively small organization with a huge mission, we consisted of very high quality personnel, which made it all work. Even though we were **"The Unit That Didn't Exist"**, we certainly contributed our fair share to winning the Cold War.

It must be understood, that we worked in a "Black Operations" mode almost all the time. This operating mode applied to our internal activities, our support to other intelligence agencies and our support to the associated overseas organizations, described in Chapter 10. Bureaucratic channels were routinely bypassed in order to get things done in an expeditious manner and to maintain security. Our security levels were well beyond

Top Secret, as was the norm for most every program related to Satellite Reconnaissance. This is the primary reason why there is very little to no documentation, still in existence, that we can refer to today. Once again, this history is based primarily on the recollections and confirmations of our remaining alumni. Official documents are presented wherever possible, but not relied upon. If not for the contributions of the dedicated people who served in our organization, our very important and significant mission would have never been revealed. We would have gone down in history as a unit that truly never existed.

Now, after all these years, the NRO has declassified the satellite programs we were associated with and we can talk about our efforts and experiences to our families, friends and the public. Due to past security constraints, many of our own members are now learning, for the first time, the details of what we actually did as a Top Secret facility. It is also very unfortunate that a good many of our members passed away before they were able to tell their families of their accomplishments. I am very thankful that we are now able to fill the knowledge gap that has existed over the years. All the families and friends of current and past alumni now know the whole story (well, almost the whole story).

Amazingly, we now exist and **"Our Mission Revealed"**.

AFSPPF Memorial Plaque

A plaque, commemorating the AFSPPF **("OUR MISSION REVEALED")** is now on display on the memorial wall, at The National Museum of the U.S. Air Force located at Wright Patterson AFB, Dayton, Ohio. This plaque reflects the mission and primary programs supported by our facility. Funds for this plaque were provided, solely, by the voluntary contributions of the many alumni of AFSPPF. The memorial wall is located outside the museum, in the Memorial Park. Following are photos of the plaque and its location within the park.

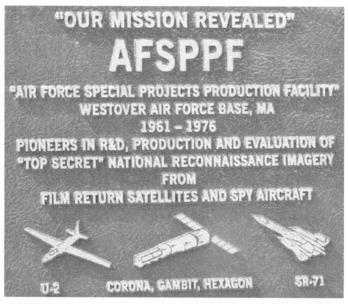

AFSPPF Memorial Plaque (July 2013) (Photo by Mike Riley)

AFSPPF Memorial Plaque Location
(Top left wall 2nd from left) (July 2013)
(Photo by Mike Riley)

AFSPPF Memorial Plaque Location – Expanded View
(Top left wall 2nd from left) (July 2013)
(Photo by Mike Riley)

National Museum of the U.S. Air Force Memorial Wall (WPAFB)
(Photo by Mike Riley)

EPILOGUE

Looking back to the early days when our unit was created, one has to ask, what were they thinking? Did they realize what we would grow to become? Now that our time has ended, we ask; what purpose did we actually serve vs. what was originally intended? How deep did our influence penetrate? Unfortunately, there are no definitive answers, other than what is presented herein.

Every member of the NRO vast team of contributors has their own stories of contributions and accomplishments. Each and every one was vital to our mission success and, since everyone worked under a cloak of secrecy; it is up to each of them to tell their own story, as they are the only ones who truly know it. I suspect the vast majority of these stories will never be told, since their people are most probably not organized or no longer alive. Perhaps some of those who read this book will become inspired and write their own. We can only hope.

As I look back and research into the past, I am finding more and more involvement of our people in ways I had no idea of at the time. It has become obvious that few, if any, of us knew the whole story of our contribution to and impact on satellite and spy aircraft reconnaissance. There are still mysteries out there that will never be revealed. As our memories are rapidly fading, we, as a group, will not live long enough, to tell the whole story.

Reflecting on the many military missions and systems development I was involved with, it has become a bit clearer as to why our unit was created, as it was. The majority of military procurements are done on a competitive basis with multiple bids being evaluated on a technical and cost basis with the most advantageous bid being funded. This all sounds great on the surface. After all, every bidder gets a fair chance to win a big government contract and make a bundle of money in the process.

Quite often, however, a smart company will learn how to bid to win, without having the ability to carry out the job. Often the low bidder gets the job; works with the contract monitor to get a change in scope of work, and then gets more money on engineering change proposals. This is often due to an improper bid that won due to a government's proposal evaluation team not understanding what was going on and just going with the low bidder. Eventually the mission gets accomplished, but with cost over runs and time extensions that delay important systems from being put into operation.

There is always plenty of blame to go around when these things happen, but with such a large bureaucracy involved, everyone still keeps their jobs and nothing is done to change the system. For those of you who have been or are involved in the government procurement system, you know exactly what I mean and I'm sure you could greatly expand on it yourself. The pros and cons could be debated forever, but the result is always the same, time delays and cost over runs. Unfortunately, the best technical solution doesn't always make it to the end product. Shuttles explode, planes crash and finger pointing begins, even with the best of intentions of all involved. These things happen with complex technical systems, so it's best to give them our best shot at the outset, with minimal political influence. Our unit was able to do this, although, we too had an occasional mishap. Something about **Murphy's Law,** I think.

I now believe the powers that be, back in the early days of establishment of the NRO and the National Reconnaissance Program, knew this fact well and decided to bypass the standard, routine procurement process in the interest of creating critical photographic intelligence on our adversaries. The concept of "Black" projects was established and the bureaucratic establishment was minimized wherever possible. Our unit was one of those organizations setup in that way and it certainly streamlined our operations. Sole source contracting was typical and where multiple bidders were involved, they were vetted beforehand. Revisit the section "R&D Contracting" in Chapter 4 for a few revealing details. Occasionally, a few bad contracts got through, but for the most part, we minimized the problem. We had the technical people capable of evaluating bids and proposals and, as mentioned previously, the snow jobs ended. We were given broad responsibility and authority to carry out our mission, with very limited oversight. Our responsibilities seemed to grow over time, as our successes accumulated. There seemed to be no end to our involvement with every satellite program. Projects and solutions moved quickly and within reasonable cost parameters. If this is what the powers that be were hoping for, it's what they got. For once, the government got it right.

We solved many problems with no credit and inspired the solution of countless others, all with no recognition. It's as if history has brushed us aside. Although silent, I now see that our contributions were far reaching, as a unit and as individuals. Yes, we did exist, but very few knew. Even though our mission is now revealed, there are still secrets out there, buried with those of us who have passed away, and there are still secrets lurking in the minds of some of us who remain, which will be left there forever. Perhaps you, as the reader of this historical work, will someday figure it all out. For now, however, this is all there is. At least should you be asked, who were those guys, you now know, **WE** were those guys.

Appendix A

Short Biographies of Major Contributors

Lloyd R. Spanberger: Author

Then   Now

Lloyd R. Spanberger was born in Detroit, MI on 15 May 1938. He graduated from Cody High School in 1956 and Graduated from Wayne State University, with a BS in Physics, in 1961. He originally majored in Electrical Engineering, but then switched to Physics allowing him to squeeze four years of study into five. The good news is, he was able to take several extra courses in the sciences and almost obtained a double degree (Physics and Math), but not quite.

During his high school days, he studied Morse code and electronics (outside of school) and obtained a General Amateur (Ham) Radio License. Prior to high school, his dad encouraged him to take up tennis as a sport, which he did, along with archery, hunting and fishing. Spring and summer months were occupied with tennis and fall and winter months were times for indoor activities, such as ham radio, making arrows for hunting, etc. and indoor badminton. All this paid off when he entered Wayne State U. Earning three varsity letters in tennis in high school prepared him for college where he earned a position on the freshman and then varsity tennis team, for three years. This paid for 50% of his tuition for the first four years of school. Ham radio paid off when he made contact with a physicist working at the Bendix Research Labs, just North of Detroit, MI. This resulted in obtaining a summer job, as a student physicist, working in a research lab. This continued until graduation, whereby he was hired on permanently, as a Junior Physicist. The work there was quite exciting, as he did research in Infrared (IR) detection and modulation and built and demonstrated a Ruby Laser from scratch.

While working at Bendix, Lloyd received a draft notice and had to report to the draft board for a physical and assignment in the US Army. He was offered an assignment to work in Army Intelligence after basic training, due to his ability to receive Morse code at over 25 words per minute and his aptitude test scores. Instead, he appealed to the draft board to allow him to apply to the Air Force Officer Training School, because of his educational background. For some mystical reason, the draft board agreed and gave him a short amount of time to apply. Ultimately, he was accepted and guaranteed an eventual assignment as a research physicist upon graduation. He entered the USAF in May of 1962, and obtained a commission as 2nd Lt in August 1962. He was subsequently assigned as a research physicist in the Infrared Reconnaissance Section, Air Force Avionics Laboratory, at Wright Patterson AFB, Dayton, OH.

This assignment was a bit unusual. Since when does the military put you where you fit in best? They actually kept their end of the bargain and the assignment fit his education and experience. He fit right in and soon assumed many responsibilities and special assignments related to the laboratory mission. He also served as a consultant to the LASER development groups in the AF, regarding LASER target designation, reconnaissance and small special weapons. He served as the AF representative on the Joint Services Coordinating Committee for Marking, Tracking and Detection, whose primary mission was to solve the many problems related to jungle warfare in Viet Nam. Many coordination meetings were held with the other branches of the service, along with ARPA, DARPA and IDA, exploring various methods of seeing and identifying targets through a dense jungle environment. A major contribution was made to the FLIR program, under project Red Sea. He contributed, significantly, to solving operational problems with that system.

Prior to completing his first year of duty, Lloyd was assigned to a special project by the Lab Commander. He was instructed to obtain infrared (IR) reconnaissance data from a vehicle flying at Mach 3 at 100,000 feet in altitude. This had never been done before and when he asked how he was supposed to do something like this, he was informed that he was an officer in the USAF and it was now his job to figure out how to get it done. The scenario that followed would make for an entire book on the subject. Over the next three years, he ultimately used the X-15 rocket plane to solve the problem and did, indeed demonstrate infrared reconnaissance at that flight profile (Actually, Mach 5 at 100,000 feet). First flight occurred in March 1965 and immediately proved the viability of IR Reconnaissance, at that flight profile. Subsequent flights were used to debug other operational problems and the program concluded in late September 1965. He was brought in on the SR-71 project "Blue Feather", which was the reason for the project in the first place. He solved the problems and made IR Reconnaissance operational in the SR-71. Ultimately, however, the IR system in the SR-71 was replaced with a SAR (Synthetic Aperture Radar) system.

The fallout from that project solved many problems with IR reconnaissance that were very beneficial to a variety of other programs. He was awarded the AF Commendation Medal for outstanding achievement, due to his development of the required IR window (which didn't exist at the time) and subsequent testing on the X-15. The SR-71 was never mentioned as part of that award. He reported directly to the Lab Commander on this project and his immediate supervisors had no idea what the ultimate goal was, which made for some very interesting situations during the course of the project. During his assignment in the IR Reconnaissance Lab, he was awarded a Masters Degree rating, due to his experience and special seminar courses he took. Upon completion of this special assignment, he was transferred to the AFSPPF at Westover AFB, as a Research Physicist, in support of Satellite Reconnaissance and Spy Aircraft programs, including the U-2 and SR-71.

He was assigned to the R&D Directorate of AFSPPF, whereby he worked on numerous projects related to the Corona, Gambit, Dorian and

Hexagon programs, as described throughout the body of this book. He was the only military physicist assigned to the R&D Directorate, during his stay there, and was involved in almost all the projects underway at that time. His primary duties were evaluation of new ideas and technical approaches and solving technical problems related to the units' mission. He personally ran an extensive test program that proved the value of dual gamma processing. Considerably effort was expended on the Dorian project, related to development of an Astronaut Training System. He chaired and attended many off site meetings involving the evaluation of a variety of techniques to accomplish this task. Ultimately, however, the program was cancelled and replaced by the Hexagon system. He coordinated with Naval Intelligence, CIA (NPIC) and Air Force Intelligence scientists on a multitude of technical matters related to advancing the state of the art in photoreconnaissance processing and analysis techniques.

Upon leaving the service, in June 1968, he worked as a physicist and engineering manager for several companies designing special purpose computers for a large variety of applications too numerous to mention. Projects involved both commercial and military systems. Lloyd eventually got into the financial services business and is now retired and living with his wife, Mary, in Mount Airy, MD. He has two daughters and five grandchildren, which keep him on his toes. His focus now is to document our unit's history, spend time traveling around this vast country, doing a little hunting and playing tennis, when possible.

Alfred (Al) C. Crane, Jr.

Then   **Now**

Alfred (Al) Charles Crane, Jr. was born in Philadelphia, PA in 1943 and was raised in Teaneck, New Jersey. He graduated from Teaneck High School in 1961. During his high school years, he also served as a cadet and sergeant in the Civil Air Patrol, Teterboro NJ Squadron, 22 Wing Air & Land Rescue Unit.

Immediately after high school, he entered The Citadel, The Military College of South Carolina, in Charleston, South Carolina. He graduated in 1965 with a BS in Physics. He was then commissioned as a 2nd Lieutenant in the US Air Force. His first assignment was at the Air Force Rocket Propulsion Lab, Edwards AFB, CA, where he served as a physicist working on the Titan 2 propellant upgrade program. He was next sent to the Tan Son Nhut AB, Vietnam in 1966.

While at Tan Son Nhut AB, he served as Shift Chief of the photo lab and Unit Security Officer of the 13th RTS (Reconnaissance Technical Squadron) and OIC of the PPIF (Photo Processing and Interpretation Facility) at the OLAA (Operating Location Alpha Alpha at Phu Cat AB) of the 460th Tactical Reconnaissance Wing. He also served as the Officer in Charge (OIC) of a self-contained mobile air force photographic processing and interpretation unit (WS430B) forward operating location detachment at Phu Cat AB.

From 1967 to 1971, he was assigned to the AFSPPF. While there, he served as the Chief of the Quality Control Division. He also provided direct support and technical assistance to many Facility & National

Intelligence Community R&D & Evaluation programs. He was directly responsible for developing the Dual Gamma processing technique with standard Wet Chemical Spray Processors, saving the Air Force millions of dollars. This technique ultimately became the standard development method for Duplicate Satellite Image Processing. Al married his wife Linda at the Base Chapel, Westover AFB, MA in Nov 1968.

From 1971 to 1976, he served as a Staff Action Officer responsible for developing standardized Quality Control Techniques and Procedures for the calibration of reconnaissance cameras, imagery production, and imagery evaluation for all USAF and ANG tactical, strategic, & national reconnaissance programs. This was accomplished by bringing the procedures developed and implemented at the AFSPPF, for National Reconnaissance Programs, "Out of the Cold" and into daily USAF SOP (Standard Operating Procedure). The program, officially named "Sentinel Sigma", was implemented by 1975. It remained in effect until photographic reconnaissance and mapping systems were phased out by digital imaging systems, in the late 1990s. He standardized management of all 21 USAF and ANG tactical reconnaissance squadron facilities and was selected as US National Representative to NATO and Allied Photographic Reconnaissance Production Standardization & interoperability Working Groups.

From 1976 to 1979, he was stationed at the HQ United States Air Forces in Europe (USAFE), Ramstein, AB, Germany as Branch Chief responsible for the management and operation of tactical reconnaissance (RF4C) Production and Armament Recording (Fighter gun camera & BDA cameras) units. He was also the USAFE representative to NATO standardization & interoperability working groups.

From 1979 to 1983, he was stationed at the Rome Air Development Center (RADC), Rome AFB, NY. While there, he served as the program manager for advanced development digital & analog reconnaissance & photogrammetric data production systems. He was selected to be a US representative to a NATO working group, on interoperability of allied tactical reconnaissance operations.

From 1983 to 1984, he was stationed at OSAN AB, Korea in the 6th Tactical Intelligence Group (TIG), as Chief Collection Manager for tasking tactical, strategic & national reconnaissance systems in support of USAF Forces in Korea operations planning, targeting, & exercise support.

From 1984 to 1987, he was assigned to the HQ Tactical Air Command (TAC), Langley AFB, VA. While there, he served as the Imagery and Intelligence Division Chief. He was responsible for managing training and operations, and integrating state of the art technology upgrades to CONUS based tactical reconnaissance production & intelligence squadrons.

Al retired from the Air Force in 1987 as a Lt Col and took a position with the Autometric Corporation, Alexandria, VA. He was a field office and program manager for application and integration of advanced national, strategic, tactical, and civil reconnaissance and remote sensing imagery systems. He served as an onsite representative for national agency, Special Operations Command, and Office of Naval Research, for the application of advanced sensors for shallow water mine detection at Air Force, Joint Command, Naval military headquarters/units, as well as on site operations manager for joint exercises at CONUS and overseas locations.

His honors and awards are as follows; Bronze Star, Vietnam; USAF Meritorious Service Medal (3X); USAF Commendation Medal; USAF Achievement Medal (Project named 'ODIN' at Griffiss AFB, NY Co-Chair/advisor to Junior Officers Council national event that brought together and honored all living USAF/AAF Medal of Honor recipients and their spouses); Special Citation from the Commander, Combat Air Command, Republic of Korea Air Forces for developing the first joint USAF/ROKAF Intelligence & reconnaissance Collection Plan; Who's Who in Optical Science & Engineering 1985; International Who's Who of Professionals 1987; Who's Who in Science & Engineering 1988-1989; Board of Directors American Society of Photogrammetry & Remote Sensing; Board of Trustees Virginia Aerospace Business Roundtable; Tidewater Chapter President, National Military Intelligence Association; Virginia Peninsula Chamber of Commerce Military Affairs Committee; Co-Chaired numerous annual National and International conferences, symposia and technical sessions and published numerous papers on Airborne Reconnaissance (SPIE), Photogrammetry and Remote Sensing (ASPRS/ISPRS) 1984-1999; Featured in Daily Press Articles Newport News, VA 6 February 2003 "Patriotic Duty-Vietnam Veteran Volunteers out of love for his Country" and 2 January 2012 "Eyes in the Sky Waged the Cold War" (Al Crane, on his classified work processing film from satellites and spy planes during the Cold War).

Al is now fully retired and living with his wife Linda in Yorktown, VA. They have a son, Alfred who served in the USMCR (Sgt), and is now civil service at US Army Training & Doctrine Command (TRADOC), Ft Eustis, near Newport News, VA.

His current activities involve serving as unit historian, AFSPPL/AFSPPF; Grace Church Yorktown VA Cemetery Committee/Memorial day/Veterans Day Ceremonies Chair Food Drive; Classic Cruisers Car Club Publicity Chair (Club raises over $12,000 annually for local charities); Historic Virginia Peninsula Region Antique Automobile Club of America, Annual Fall Round up Chair; City of Newport News VA, Archaeology Volunteer.

James (Jim) O. Grimm

Then   Now

James (Jim) Orval Grimm was born 23 April 1928 in Bucyrus, Ohio. At 16 years old, he began working part-time in local factories as an apprentice machinist, supporting World War II efforts. He attended Bucyrus High School and graduated in May 1946. He has a Bachelor's degree in Business and Masters Degree in Management Science, in addition to extensive formal Air Force Photo Engineer and Science training.

Jim received an Army draft notice in 1945 at 17½ years old while a senior in high school. Signing on with the Army Air Corps versus the Army allowed him to complete high school. He spent 19 years of his Air Force career of 26 years in foreign countries (13 years in the Pacific Far East and 6 years in Western Europe).

Supporting top-secret aerial reconnaissance and undercover intelligence activities in different parts of the world was Jim's forte. He traveled extensively in the Far East as a photoreconnaissance technical advisor to allied foreign governments, while secretly obtaining intelligence information for the United States Government.

In 1963, he was selected by the Department of Defense (DOD) to manage the Air Force's top-secret precision photo processing laboratory for the Corona spy satellite program; involving the processing and reproduction of critical imagery collected over Russia and other communist countries during the Cold War.

During this assignment to the covert 6594th Test Squadron (later known as AFSPPF), his management, engineering, and photo science abilities significantly assisted the Air Force and Government intelligence agencies in developing and establishing advanced technology for processing top secret imagery collected by spy satellites and long-range high altitude aircraft such as the U-2 and SR-71. He was especially adept in design, construction, and management of precision photo processing and reproduction laboratories.

Jim provided photo intelligence processing support during the Berlin Crisis, Lebanon Conflict, Korean War, Southeast Asia War, Occupation of Japan, and Taiwan Strait Conflict.

His military awards and decorations are as follows: Army Good Conduct Medal; World War II Victory Medal; Japan Occupation Medal; Meritorious Unit Citation Medal; Korean Service Medal; United Nations Service Medal; Air Force Outstanding Unit Award; Air Force Commendation Medal; Non-Commissioned Officer Academy Ribbon; National Defense Service Medal; Air Force Longevity Service Award; Air Force Good Conduct Medal; Cold War Recognition Certificate; Armed Forces Expeditionary Medal; Distinguished Unit Citation; Presidential Unit Citation; Small Arms Expert Ribbon; US-Republic of China Mutual Defense Commemorative Medal and USAF Photo School Engineering Honors.

Jim retired from the United States Air Force 30 September 1972 as a Chief Master Sergeant and immediately accepted a management/engineering position with General Electric Company's (GE) Aero Space Division in Maryland. As an employee/contractor, with top-secret security clearances, he provided management and engineering services to Government agencies involved with spy, environmental, and earth resource satellites. Under a GE contract with the National Aeronautics and Space Administration (NASA), located in MD, he assisted NASA in acquiring and producing millions of high resolution Landsat Satellite images of earth resources. His establishment of advanced quality control procedures and defect monitoring activities within a clean room environment contributed significantly to the production of high quality imagery used for scientific research, and for developing policies for protecting national resources from destruction caused by environmental disturbances. Landsat imagery was also valuable for planning and discovery of new resources such as oil, natural gas, and water.

Under an additional GE contract with the National Oceanic and Atmospheric Administration's (NOAA) National Environment Satellite, Data, and Information Service (NESDIS), located in MD, Jim managed the production of GOES (Geostationary Operational Environmental Satellite) imagery, used widely 24/7 by Government intelligence agencies (CIA, FBI, DOD), universities, climatology research laboratories, and radio and television studios. This vital information was widely disseminated and contributed significantly to the safety and welfare of the public sector in terms of weather warnings for flooding, hurricanes, tornadoes, and other environmental issues.

As project engineer/manager working with the Central Intelligence Agency (CIA/NRO) from 1986-1993, Jim designed, monitored construction, equipped, staffed, and managed a 3,000 square foot multi-million dollar top secret space satellite imagery processing and reproduction facility. He secretly worked with CIA officials and analysts of the National Photographic Interpretation Center (NPIC) in the collection, processing, and dissemination of top-secret, spy satellite intelligence data used to determine different levels of defense and policies for national security. Timely intelligence was provided to the President, Pentagon, Defense Intelligence Agency (DIA) and overseas Battle Field Commanders.

Jim's 47 years of combined military and civilian service in advancing satellite imagery collection, processing and production technologies contributed significantly to the nation's national security and Cold War intelligence programs. His endeavors in the public sector after military retirement were substantial and instrumental in providing scientific research data for effective management and development of national resources, and for providing safety for the American people during severe environmental disturbances.

Jim finally retired in 1993 and settled down in Florida with his wife, Patricia. The stock market, genealogy, memoir writing, visiting grandchildren, and yard work keeps him busy.

Samuel (Sam) D. McCulloch

Then   Now

Sam was born on a small farm and ranch, 30 June 1934, in the area of Aransas Pass, Texas. He graduated from high school at the age of 16 and attended TCU (Texas Christian University) in Fort Worth. He worked his way through, mostly washing dishes in a commercial cafeteria. He was commissioned in the USAF as a 2nd Lieutenant in May 1955, after completing his BA in geology with a minor in biology. The AFROTC program at TCU required entry into the pilot training program; however, passing the eye test was not to be and he was sent to the Air and Ground Photography School at Lowry AFB, Denver, CO. He was then assigned to the Photographic Lab of the 2nd RTS at Barksdale AFB, Louisiana, and ultimately to the Photo Interpretation Branch, managing a team of photo interpreters in preparing intelligence reports for use in producing air target charts. He was promoted to 1st Lieutenant during this assignment.

After getting married to Anita Jackson and having their first child, he extended his 3-year active duty commitment, resulting in his assignment to the 67th RTS at Yokota Air Base, Japan, as a P.I. (Photo Interpreter). During the first two years or so, he managed a P.I. team interpreting air photos covering various parts of China, using conventional aircraft and cameras.

In the fall of 1959, he became part of a small group of P.I.'s who received special clearances and worked in a secure facility preparing reports from images obtained by U-2's. Briefings were held before each set of missions by two individuals from NPIC. These missions concerned flights over Laos, North and South Vietnam. He was promoted to Captain before leaving the organization.

He began his assignment with the 6594th TS/AFSPPL, Westover AFB, in Jan 1962, as a P.I. in the Operations Directorate. Several months later, he was assigned to the PET (Performance Evaluation Team), then under the R&D Directorate, evaluating the quality of imagery from photoreconnaissance satellites that were in the R&D phase. Additional duties, during his four years in the facility, included one interesting effort as executive secretary to a special photo intelligence committee that was developing overseas capabilities suitable for supporting national-level requirements. The committee was responsible for establishing a part of the 67th RTS in Japan as the first such facility, the same secure area in which he had worked during his assignment there. He traveled with AFSPPL commander, Col. Harold Ohlmeyer, who was chairman of the committee, to and from the Pentagon for several weeks, until the committee agreed to the facility identified as OPIC-A. The NPIC representative to the committee was the person he had worked with on the U-2 missions, while in the 67th RTS.

Sam left AFSPPF in December 1965, and entered the Geodetic Sciences MS program at Ohio State. With an MS degree under his belt and a promotion to Major, he was soon assigned as Chief of Intelligence for the 388th Tactical Fighter Wing at Korat, Thailand. While there, he expanded the group from five to six branches to include one that focused on Escape and Evasion. As an aside, the Deputy Director of Operations was the famous West Point football player, Doc Blanchard, then a full colonel. He was often asked to take visitors to meet Col. Blanchard, especially if they were about his age or older, and the visitors told him later that this act alone made their trip to his office a complete success.

In 1968, he was assigned to the DIA (Defense Intelligence Agency) at the Pentagon. He was assigned to DIAXX, which dealt with photoreconnaissance projects, including those at the national level. He served as a member of several National-level committees that met periodically at NPIC, including a national-level Color Committee, for which he conducted a survey of military organizations worldwide, to determine their capabilities for handling color imagery. The results were compiled and submitted as part of a report on possible future uses of color imagery in photoreconnaissance satellite programs.

Various other assignment offers developed during his stay at DIA and then he eventually received a request from Al Crane, then at USAF HQ in the Pentagon, asking that he chair an Air-Force-Wide committee on developing a manual for conducting image evaluations in the reconnaissance photo labs that could lead to improved performance. He conducted several meetings of the group that included representatives from NPIC and the Rome Air Development Center, as well as individuals from recon tech units located overseas and stateside. He was able to develop an outline and draft part of the document, but was reassigned to the DIA before its completion. The image evaluation manual was eventually completed and a USAF regulation on image evaluation had been implemented based on it. He was promoted to Lt Col during this assignment. He retired from the USAF in August 1975.

During his last assignment with the DIA, Sam and his wife, Anita participated in an evening course on archeology that included fieldwork. This resulted in their development of a great interest in pursuing archeology when they got back to Texas, specifically to Austin. It took about eleven years attending the University of Texas part time to get an MS in archeology in May 1986. During these years, he worked for the TWDB (Texas Water Development Board). As part of his work there, he drafted a bill to make the newly established TNRIS (Texas National resources Information System) a formal part of State government, which was then approved by the Governor. This effort at TNRIS was simply an application of his experiences in the Air Force. TNRIS was oriented around data categories within the natural environment and one area; identified as Base Data; essentially dealt with aerial photos, space imagery and cartographic materials, which was his primary area of responsibility.

Within a few years, TNRIS became well known throughout many of the states as well as several foreign countries, with individuals visiting the staff to learn how to develop a similar system in their own states or countries. Sam presented numerous talks on the System over the eleven years he worked there, including a presentation in Seattle to about 300 participants, where he received an award, on behalf of TNRIS, from the Urban and Regional Information Systems Association. He visited the NASA facility near Houston many times to coordinate a joint effort for evaluating state agency uses of the new Landsat imagery, as a part of NASA's technology transfer program. At the same time that his work at TNRIS was proceeding so well, Anita and he became active in the archeological community. Shortly, after joining a local organization, Sam was soon elected President, whereby they both became even more involved in that field of endeavor.

During the summer of 1986, Sam resigned from TNRIS and began work on archeological projects for several companies, agencies, and one university, managing various projects during the next 25 years. Anita worked with him in the field, in the lab, and in the office until her death from cancer in 1999. They had four children. In 2004, he began his own company, McCulloch Archeological Services LLC, but closed it at the end of 2012.

Appendix B

Short Biography of the Original AFSPPF Commander

Harold Z. Ohlmeyer was born on October 1, 1919 in Franklin, LA. He passed away on September 22, 2010 at the age of 91. He attended college at Saint Mary's University in San Antonio, Texas where he played football, tennis and was the tri state lightweight boxing champion for two years. He entered the Army Air Corps in January 1942, after the US was attacked at Pearl Harbor, and was commissioned a 2nd Lieutenant. He was trained as a bombardier and he flew 51 combat missions in North Africa and Italy from December 1943 to December 1944. During these missions, he achieved one of the highest bomb scoring percentages in the US Air Force.

He married his wife Sylvia Irene Matthews of Eden, Mississippi on December 29, 1944. They subsequently, had three children, Beverly, Bill and Ronald. From this point on, he served in a variety of Air Force Administrative, training and staff positions, including a short stay with NATO in Paris, France. He ultimately settled in at Westover AFB, as Deputy Director, Training Division, HQ 8th Air Force, in June of 1955. He became the Director of the 8th RTS, Westover AFB, MA in May 1957. This unit was responsible for producing, among other things, radar and aerial photos, target charts, mosaics and related materials for SAC. He established several changes in production techniques, which resulted in quadrupling production.

Col Ohlmeyer transitioned to Commander of the AFSPPL (Air Force Satellite Photographic Processing Laboratory) in February 1961, when the 6594th TS moved into building 1900, on base, following the Secretary of the Air Force establishment of the AFSPPL. He was able to acquire certain personnel and equipment from the 8th RTS to begin the setup of this high tech photo lab. He remained as commander when the facility became HQ Air Force Special Projects Production Facility in November 1965. He worked closely with the Secretary of the Air Force, CIA, NRO and other DOD intelligence agencies, during the early days of Satellite and Aerospace Reconnaissance, to establish a highly qualified facility to provide R&D and photographic production services for these highly classified systems. He was responsible for staffing the facility with highly qualified individuals and acquiring the best state of the art equipment, to get the job done.

He commanded the facility during the days of U-2 missions and SR-71 development, as well as supporting the SAMOS, Corona and Gambit satellite programs. The unit was awarded the Air Force Outstanding Unit Award, during his tenure there. In the three months prior to his retirement, in August 1968, he also served as Special Assistant to the Deputy Director for Satellite Programs.

He received the following military decorations: Legion of Merit, Distinguished Flying Cross with Oak Leaf Cluster, Air Medal with four Oak Leaf Clusters, Air Force Commendation Medal, Presidential Unit Citation Award, Air Force Outstanding Unit Award, American Campaign Medal, European-African-Middle Eastern Campaign Medal, WWII Victory Medal, National Defense Service Medal with Oak Leaf Cluster and the Air Force Longevity Medal with Silver Oak leaf Cluster.

Upon retirement, Colonel Ohlmeyer, his wife Irene and his son Ronald moved to Yazoo city, Mississippi. While in Yazoo City, he served as headmaster at Manchester Academy and then headmaster at Cruger-Tchula Academy. Later, he worked for the State in the Mental Health program, running the County office in Yazoo City and then, the District office in Vicksburg. He loved to play golf at the Yazoo City Country Club and fish in a secret place. Colonel Ohlmeyer and his son Ronald attended the 2004 AFSPPF reunion in Bay, Saint Louis, MS.

Appendix C

Copies of declassified original NRO documents related to our organization

TOP SECRET TCS-9784-61-KH

THE WHITE HOUSE
Washington

August 26, 1960

MEMORANDUM FOR

The Secretary of State
The Secretary of Defense*
The Attorney General**
The Chairman, Atomic Energy Commission
The Director of Central Intelligence

I hereby direct that the products of satellite reconnaissance, and information of the fact of such reconnaissance revealed by the product,
shall be given strict security handling under the provisions of a
special security control system approved by me. I hereby approve
the TALENT-KEYHOLE Security Control System for this purpose.

Within your agency, you shall be personally responsible for the selection of those personnel who will have access to the foregoing information
and for determining the scope of that access. Access is to be on a
"must know" basis related to major national security needs. A list of
those selected shall be furnished to the Director of Central Intelligence,
who will maintain and review the control roster. When they are in-
doctrinated, they shall be informed of my specific direction to them
that the provisions of the special Security Control System I have
approved be strictly complied with, including the prohibition upon them
of imparting any information within this system to any person not specifically known to them to be on the list of those authorized to receive
this material. The responsibility for the selection of personnel may
be delegated only to the senior intelligence chief or chiefs within the
agencies serving as members of the U. S. Intelligence Board.

The Director of Central Intelligence, in consultation with the U. S.
Intelligence Board, will be responsible to me for determining all questions involved in the continued protection and control of the foregoing
material and information, including the development of a common
understanding as to the meaning of the term " 'must know' basis related to major national security needs," and a broad consensus as to
the numbers of personnel in each agency comprehended by this term.

*For Department of Defense   signed Dwight D. Eisenhower
including OSD, JCS, Army,
Navy, Air Force, and NSA   HANDLE VIA TALENT-
**For Director, FBI   KEYHOLE SYSTEM ONLY

TOP SECRET   TN 3462-61KH
SERIES A.

CONFIDENTIAL

NO: 116.2
DATE: December 15, 1960

SECRETARY OF THE AIR FORCE
ORDER

SUBJECT: Organization and Functions of the Air Force
Satellite Photographic Processing Laboratory

1. There is hereby established the Air Force Satellite
Photographic Processing Laboratory (AFSPPL) at Westover Air
Force Base, Massachusetts.

2. The Laboratory will be under the command of the
Director of the SAMOS Project, 2400 East El Segundo Boulevard,
El Segundo, California. It will be attached to the Air Force
Command and Control Development Division, Air Research and
Development Command, L. G. Hanscom Field, Massachusetts, for
administrative, logistic, and contractual support.

3. The mission of the AFSPPL will be to conduct the
research and development necessary to provide the best possible
equipment, techniques, and knowledge applicable to satellite
photography, to insure that the processing and duplication of
photography obtained from satellite vehicles is of the highest
possible quality, and to process, duplicate, and distribute
this photography to designated users.

4. Physical space and some resources and manning for the
AFSPPL will be taken from the 8th Reconnaissance Technical
Squadron. The 8th Reconnaissance Technical Squadron will

SAFSR D.

CONFIDENTIAL

AFHQ FORM 0-841. 17 APR 53

CONFIDENTIAL

NO: 116.2
DATE: December 15, 1960

remain as a separate unit, with the AFSPPL having priority over all resources. Actual transfer of spaces, manpower, and other resources will follow approval of a detailed plan to be submitted to the Secretary of the Air Force by the Director of the SAMOS Project.

Dudley C. Sharp

2

CONFIDENTIAL

FOR OFFICIAL USE ONLY

NO: 116.3

DATE: August 25, 1964

SECRETARY OF THE AIR FORCE
ORDER

SUBJECT: Organization and Function of the Air Force Special Projects Production Laboratory

1. There is hereby established the Air Force Special Projects Production Laboratory (AFSPPL) (U) at Westover Air Force Base, Massachusetts.

2. The Laboratory will be under the command of the Director of Special Projects, OSAF, 2400 East El Segundo Boulevard, El Segundo, California. It will be assigned organizationally to the 6594th Aerospace Test Wing (AFSC), Sunnyvale, California. Host base will provide support in accordance with AFR 11-4.

3. The mission of the AFSPPL will be to conduct the research and development necessary to provide the best possible production equipment and techniques in support of special projects specified by the Secretary of the Air Force.

EUGENE M. ZUCKERT
Secretary of the Air Force

FOR OFFICIAL USE ONLY

TOP SECRET

(S) NATIONAL RECONNAISSANCE OFFICE
WASHINGTON, D.C.

OFFICE OF THE DIRECTOR

October 23, 1973

MEMORANDUM FOR GENERAL MEYER, SAC

SUBJECT: Production Facility for Satellite Photography

We have recently discussed the possibility of relocating some of the functions of the Air Force Special Projects Production Facility to the 544th ARTW at Offutt AFB. I have decided to close the AFSPPF and move a portion of the satellite reconnaissance photographic duplication function to the 544th ARTW. Should the primary facility become unavailable, this will provide a suitable backup capability for processing satellite photography.

I recognize that this decision will require a significant modification to the present facility occupied by the 544th ARTW. Until these modifications are complete, I plan to maintain a capability at Westover Air Force Base. I wish to proceed quickly to develop implementing plans and ask that you name a point of contact. The contact on my staff is Brigadier General John E. Kulpa, Jr., SAFSS, who may be reached at OX 7-8675 or Command Post drop 647.

John L. McLucas

cc: Chief of Staff

TOP SECRET

CONTROL N°   3214-73
COPY 3 OF _____ COPIES
PAGE 1 OF 1 PAGES

~~TOP SECRET~~

~~(S)~~ NATIONAL RECONNAISSANCE OFFICE
WASHINGTON, D.C.

THE NRO STAFF   November 27, 1973

MEMORANDUM FOR MR. CARL DUCKETT, CIA

SUBJECT: NRO Photographic System Evaluation Functions

As you are aware, the Department of Defense announced earlier this year that Westover Air Force Base, Massachusetts, will be closed except for certain designated units including the Air Force Special Projects Production Facility (AFSPPF). For several reasons, it has now been decided to relocate the functions performed by the AFSPPF and eventually close the facility.

One function which must continue to be performed is that of photographic system evaluation, and we favor moving this activity to the National Photographic Interpretation Center (NPIC). Informal discussions with NPIC have shown that the functions in question are closely related to those presently being performed, and that the capability can be augmented to assume the additional workload.

The Director, NPIC, is willing to assume this additional function. Manpower spaces, qualified people, and existing equipment would be transferred to NPIC by the NRO sometime in late FY 1975 or FY 1976 as the AFSPPF is phased down. With your concurrence, we will proceed to firm up and formalize our planning. I would ▮▮▮▮▮▮▮▮▮▮▮▮▮▮▮▮▮▮▮▮▮▮▮▮ with you.

JOHN E. ▮▮▮▮▮▮▮, JR.
Brigadier General, USAF
Director

 ~~TOP SECRET~~

~~TOP SECRET~~

(S) NATIONAL RECONNAISSANCE OFFICE
WASHINGTON, D.C.

THE NRO STAFF

1 6 OCT 1974

MEMORANDUM FOR MR. PLUMMER

SUBJECT: Relocation of the Photo R&D Function of the Air Force
Special Projects Production Facility (AFSPPF)

The closure of AFSPPF and the relocation of its tasks
are proceeding on schedule. There remains two items to be
closed out which will complete the decision-making process
and allow final programming. First is the final decision
on the location of the Photo R&D function and second is the
reply to General Keegan's (AF/IN) letter of 15 July 1974
(Atch 1) which suggests that all of the functions of the
AFSPPF be integrated at SAC in Omaha, Nebraska. General Kulpa
addressed both of these items in his 25 July 1974 memo to
you (Atch 2) which he indicated that the Evaluation function
had received approval from all participants to be relocated
at the NPIC and that commitments and planning had already been
accomplished. In the same memo he provided you information as
to the progress made in reaching an agreement for the Photo R&D,
but that he felt it was too premature to make a decision until
he and General Bradburn had an opportunity to fully analyze
the problem.

In your memo to General Kulpa on 26 July 1974 (Atch 3),
you agreed with the relocation of the Evaluation function to
the NPIC and also indicated that you desired that both
General Kulpa and General Bradburn include in their analysis
the option of placing the Photo R&D function at Omaha.

Numerous discussions between the SAFSS/SP staffs have
taken place along with discussions with OD&E people. A
portion of the success and fulfillment of the tasks undertaken
at AFSPPF has been in cooperation with the Evaluation function
utilizing their instrumentation and skilled technicians.

 ~~TOP SECRET~~

CONTROL NO Internal
COPY 1 OF 2 COPIES
PAGE 1 OF 2 PAGES

TOP SECRET

Also the QC lab which provides all QC/QA functions for R&D
is available. With the separation of functions, this type
of support creates an atmosphere which requires more support
in the form of duplicate equipment and the necessity to have
additional manpower to provide the desired results. This
type analysis was accomplished with the basic thought and
goal to resolve the situation in a manner which is most
beneficial to the NRP as well as being the most cost effective.

Both General Bradburn and General Kulpa agreed that the
most advantageous placement would be in the Washington, D.C.
area to be melded with the Program B Imagery Technology Division.
This has the advantage of placing both the photo and exploitation
R&D efforts together which best serves the NRP as well as
utilizing common facilities and equipment.

The proviso remains that if a specific photo R&D task is
best served by placing it with the program manager in Los
Angeles, that this should be done. The overall direction
will be from the NRO Configuration Change Board (CCB) which
has three members representing SAF/SS, SAFSP and ODG&E. In
this manner the most cost effective and program satisfaction
criteria can be applied to the specific task being undertaken.

The message on the right sets forth a common ground of
understanding to create both a home and direction for the
photo R&D function. I want to make clear that General Kulpa,
General Bradburn and Mr. Les Dirks have all seen this message
and that all three have agreed to its contents.

Request you release the message on the right as well as
the letter to General Keegan informing him of the placement
of both the Evaluation and Photo R&D functions of the AFSPPF.

Colonel, USAF
Director

3 Atch
1. Gen Keegan Ltr
2. Gen Kulpa Memo
3. Mr. Plummer Memo

TOP SECRET

CONTROL SYSTEM

CONTROL NO_____
COPY___ OF___ COPIES
PAGE 2 OF 2 PAGES

Appendix D

AFSPPF Origination memo from Maxwell AFB

Subj: **RE: Air Force Special Projects Production Facility**
Date: 6/26/02 3:03:02 PM Eastern Daylight Time
From: Horace.Carson@MAXWELL.AF.MIL
To: CraneJrA@aol.com
Sent from the Internet (Details)

Dear LtCol Crane:

I am unable to find any information in our holdings regarding the Air Force Special Projects Laboratory (afsppl).

However, I did find information in our holdings regarding the Air Force Special Projects Production Facility.

The HQ, Air Force Special Projects Production Facility was constituted, activated, and assigned to the Air Force Systems Command for organization on or about 10 Nov 1965 at Westover AFB, Chicopee Falls, Mass. Upon organization was further assigned to the Space Systems Division. On or about 1 Jul 1967 the Facility was released from the Space Systems Division and assigned to the Space and Missile Systems Organization. On or about 1 Jan 1977, the HQ Air Force Special Projects Production Facility was inactivated.

According to the AFP 900-2 Volume II (23 Nov 1981), The Air Force Special Projects Production Facility was awarded the Air Force Organizational Excellence Award (AFOEA) for the following periods:
   1 Jul 71 - 30 Jun 72
   1 Jul 74 - 30 Jun 76

Should you have further questions or require additional information, please email them to afhranews@maxwell.af.mil. Please Cc me on the request.

Thank you again for your inquiry, and we wish you success with your reunion.

Appendix E

Acknowledgment of our organization by the NRO

NATIONAL RECONNAISSANCE OFFICE
14675 Lee Road
Chantilly, VA 20151-1715

Office of the Director

30 August 2002

Lieutenant Colonel Alfred C. Crane, Jr. USAF (Ret)
AFSPPF/6594th TS 2002 Reunion
104 Winder Road
Tabb, VA 23693

To the Alumni of the AFSPPF/6594th Test Squadron:

On the occasion of the 6594th Test Squadron's 2002 reunion, I wish to
recognize all the members of the unit for their important contributions to the
success of the Cold War-era Corona photoreconnaissance program.

The Corona program claims many "firsts": the world's first photo
reconnaissance satellite, the first mid-air recovery of a vehicle returning
from space, the first mapping of earth from space, the first stereo-optical
data acquired from space, and the first use of multiple reentry vehicles from
space. Moreover, Corona and the people responsible for the program set the
standards of excellence for which ensuing generations of scientists, engineers,
intelligence analysts, and support elements continue to strive.

When considering the remarkable capabilities of today's reconnaissance
satellites, it is easy to lose sight of how revolutionary Corona's technology
was in the 1950s. Yet 1-meter resolution, near-real-time returns, and the
dramatic increase in mission duration are simply improvements on the technology
that Corona pioneered.

The role of the 6594th Test Squadron, and later the Air Force Special
Projects Production Facility (AFSPPF), was to produce and ship roll-duplicate
positive film and selected products to Corona exploitation centers. This was
no small undertaking, considering that during the 12 years that Corona operated, it returned 2.1 million feet of film in 39,000 cans! The AFSPPF also
played an important role in the technical evaluation and analysis for each
Corona mission-initiating many innovation quality control and production
techniques for the program.

The alumni of the 6594th Test Squadron and AFSPPF have every reason to be
very proud of the role they played in the absolute success of the Corona
satellite program and its contributions to our national security. I wish the
best to each of you.

Sincerely,

Peter B. Teets

NATIONAL RECONNAISSANCE OFFICE
14675 Lee Road
Chantilly, VA 20151-1715

19 October 2006

THE 6594th TEST SQUADRON
On The Occasion of Your 2006 Reunion

To a Generation of Sentinels,

On behalf of my colleagues at the National
Reconnaissance Office (NRO), I extend our appreciation to
the members of the 6594th Test Squadron for your
contributions to national security during the Cold War, and
I congratulate you on the occasion of your reunion.

The Cold War was a historical period that made America
and the whole world hold a collective breath. With the
threat of nuclear attacks always present, tensions were at
a constant high. One of the most valuable capabilities the
U.S. had at that time was its intelligence and
reconnaissance systems. Early national reconnaissance
systems played critical roles in helping U.S. decision
makers accurately assess Soviet and Warsaw Pact
capabilities and intentions. Human source intelligence
activities were constrained by the Iron Curtain; and
signals intelligence from the Grab and Poppy satellites
helped paint part of the picture. But a key component to
America's successful intelligence enterprises during the
Cold War was the collection, processing, and analysis of
reconnaissance film in support of imagery intelligence
(imint). America's imint output showed intelligence
analysts, policymakers, and strategists exactly what was
happening in denied areas, and produced a clearer picture
of the Soviet threat.

The 6594th Test Squadron, serving at the Air Force
Special Projects Production Facility, played an integral
role in the production and technical evaluation of imagery
acquired by the Corona KH-4 imagery intelligence system.
From 20 February 1961 through 1 January 1977, 6594th
squadron personnel at Westover Air Force Base processed the

film recovered in Corona capsules, and sent the imagery to centers and agencies for analysis.

The work of the 6594th Test Squadron was invaluable to the success of the Corona program during a critical period in American history. Your dedication to duty and resolve deserve the highest of praise. All of you are trailblazers in the evolution of national reconnaissance. Thanks to your efforts, not only is this country safer, but your example has inspired new generations of analysts and technical experts to search for and find new ways to advance the discipline of imagery intelligence. Your contributions laid the foundation for one of the crucial elements of today's intelligence capability.

Thank you for your contributions to national security, for laying the foundation of the art and science of imagery intelligence processing, and for your critical role in helping the U.S. win the Cold War.

Sincerely,

Robert A. McDonald
Director, Center for the Study of
National Reconnaissance
Business Plans and Operations
National Reconnaissance Office

NATIONAL RECONNAISSANCE OFFICE
14675 Lee Road
Chantilly, VA 20151-1715

Office of the Director

12 October 2011

Lieutenant Colonel Alfred C. Crane, Jr.,
   USAF (Ret)
AFSPPF/6594TS 2011 Reunion
104 Winder Road
Tabb, VA 23693

Dear Colonel Crane:

   Thank you, Colonel Crane and Alumni members of the 659ᵗʰ Test
Squadron/Air Force Special Project Production Facility for your
critical contributions to the National Reconnaissance Office (NRO) and
our nation's security.

   Your work in the satellite film-return programs directly
contributed to America's supremacy in space and ultimately led us to
victory in the Cold War. Your patriotism and dedication gave America
the ability to monitor compliance with key international agreements
and treaties and made the NRO the primary source of intelligence about
denied areas. We could not have done this without your willing
sacrifices.

   My recent declassification of two of our historic programs,
GAMBIT and HEXAGON, has lifted the secrecy surrounding some of your
work, and I hope your families and friends will now be able to
appreciate the value of your innovative contributions and the
complexity of the challenges you faced. Specifically, your work in
processing and disseminating the tremendous volume of exposed film in
all the film-return satellite programs was essential to providing the
military key information and gave decision makers the insights needed
to effectively deal with our adversaries from a position of strength.

   Congratulations to all on a job well done.

                         Sincerely,

                         Bruce Carlson

Appendix F

AFSPPF Reunion Photos

AFSPPF Alumni and NRO Display
1. Lou Falconieri, 2. Graydon Hudspeth, 3. Carl Lind, 4. George Myers, 5. Richard F. Wagner,
6. Peter Thorpe, 7. George White, 8. Larry Mathews, 9. Roger Glascock, 10. Herb Duval,
11. Robert Finnegan, 12. Bill Happel, 13. Bill Dishon, 14. Joe Laurendi, 15. Allen Scott,
16. Mac McBrayer, 17. Leroy Coulter, 18. Joe Lenihan, 19. Lee Colville, 20. Archie Smith,
21. Russ Sanner, 22. Bill Topper, 23. Charlie Jennings, 24. Ray Smith, 25. Richard D. Wagner,
26. Bob Borak, 27. Tom Shacklett, 28. Bill Broome, 29. Raul Santiago, 30. Dennis Sage,
31. Bill Ray, 32. Leroy Miller, 33. Hal Gordon, 34. James Blackwell, 35. Lynn Harris,
36. Obbie Ezzel, 37. Robert Sisson, 38. Natalie Harmon, 39. Gordon Pritchard,
40. George Berryman, 41. William Tulloch, 42. Jim Grimm, 43. Al Crane, 44. Ed Bryk
Missing reunion members: John Hilten, Joe Powers, Wayne Smith, Bill Valentine, Darrell Krause,
Robert Travers, Rich McLaughlin, John Vooris, Renata Grochal, and Bud Wrest.

First AFSPPF Alumni Reunion October 2002
(Photo by Flash Photo, Branson, MO)

Air Force Special Projects Production Facility
Corona Program Reunion
Myrtle Beach, SC October 23-27, 2006

Front Row (L-R): Leroy (Moose) Miller, Jim Grimm, Al Crane, Herb Duval, George Myers, Bill Ray, Bill Dishon.
Back Row (L-R): Bob Jewell, Ed Harris, Lee Colville, Roger Glascock, Russ Sinner, Joe Lenihan, Dick Temple,
Ric Wagner, Bob Borak, Mac McBrayer, George White, Dick Wagner

AFSPPF Alumni Reunion, October 2006 (Photo by Gene Ho)

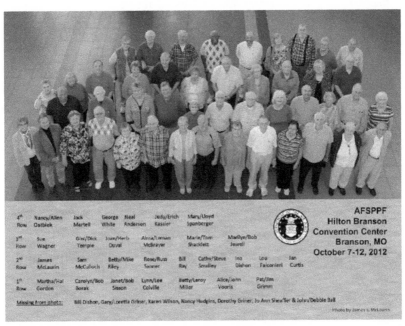

AFSPPF Alumni Reunion, October 2012 (Photo by James E. McLaurin)

Appendix G

Select List of Members

The following members of AFSPPF and related organizations have contributed to the information presented in this historical document.

Jack Anderson, MSgt, Power Production Section from 1970–1974

See Chapter 2 for reference to Jacks contribution. He recalls the following experiences:

"Probably the strangest thing I recall was the diesel electric generators, installed in late 1970, were from missile site 5A at Lowry AFB, and I was the power plant NCOIC just before SAC closed down the Titan Missile program at Lowry. I went from there to Vietnam in 65-66 then 4 years in 6910th Security service in Germany, only to end up at Westover in charge of the same generators. If my memory serves me correctly, the power plant operators were the only ones to wear white coveralls."

William C. Dishon, SMSgt, Photo Lab Operations from 1963–1966

Bill's job Responsibilities included NCOIC Chemical Analysis, NCOIC inside Sensitometry and Shift Supervisor of the Photo Lab Division. His accomplishments were, as follows: Mainly contributing to the overall accomplishment of the mission. Much of the time was spent in the relative obscurity of the night shift (6:00 PM to 6:00 AM). One accomplishment may be noteworthy. At one point, Eastman Kodak Company stopped supplying the developer used in our processors. Using the analytical lab on site, he was able to analyze their developer, and duplicate their formula within a fraction of a g/l (gram per liter). This enabled us to keep operating and complete the mission. After leaving AFSPPF, he served as Course Supervisor of the Precision Photo Courses (234XX) at Lowry AFB. In this capacity, he continued to contribute to the organization by identifying students for Col. Taylor (Facility Security Officer) who might be aptly skilled and able to withstand the investigation for security clearance, for assignment to AFSPPF.

Raymond L. Ferland, TSgt, Operations Div, Special Activities from 1970–1974

Raymond provided support for all classified communications for all projects associated with AFSPPF.

Joe Franklin, MSgt, Technical Analysis Div. from 1961–1963

Joe entered the Air Force in 1941 and served in many photo related capacities throughout his career. He was assigned to the U-2 Project, 4080th SRW in October 1956 as NCOIC of their Mission Critique Office, first at Turner AFB, Albany GA, and then at Laughlin AFB, Del Rio, TX. He was subsequently assigned to the 67th RTS, Yokota, Japan, where he served as a Photo Interpreter. He was eventually transferred to the AFSPPL in 1961. While working in our facility, he was instrumental in developing the "Edge Gradient" method of determining resolution of early satellite imagery.

Harold Gordon, Col, Asst Chief Evaluation Div from 1969-1973

Hal Supervised technical personnel, in providing subjective/objective and pre-/post- flight analysis of CORONA, GAMBIT and HEXAGON photoreconnaissance satellite systems. He coordinated deployment of Controlled Range Network (CORN) targets across the US for tri-bar, edge, tri-color and gray scale target mensuration. He later served as a Deputy Director in the NRO and Deputy Chief of Staff/Intelligence, Air Force Space Command. He contributed significantly to the brainstorming sessions, during our reunion in 2012.

Richard D. Hale, Capt, R&D Div from 1966-1969

Dick's responsibilities included creating the automated product tracking programs for the production lab, using an IBM 1130 computer.

That transitioned into a project to develop a feedback control system for the developer machines in the production lab, using an IBM 1800 computer. He was successful in implementing both systems. He also supported the contract tracking and maintenance for the various R&D contractors supporting the facility.

Erich Kassler, TSgt, 497th RTG Technical Analysis Div from 1955-1960

Erich contributed the Rhine River Patrol story related in Chapter 10. He also contributed to our brainstorming sessions, during our reunion in 2012. While stationed at Lindsey Air Base in Wiesbaden Germany, he was captain of the Volleyball team. They became the base champions and traveled to many different countries and areas representing the Air Force. They won against all teams except the French. He recalls they had very few tall players, but they could jump like frogs. It turns out that, since sport teams got to travel a lot, they were often used as couriers and contact points, for low level Intelligence.

Leman V. McBrayer, TSgt, NCOIC Printing and Q/C from 1962-1971

Richard U. Miller, SSgt, 8th RTS Photo Interpreter from 1955-1957

Richards's job was the preliminary interpretation of aerial photography, the preparation of intelligence material for dissemination and the updating of target charts. He exercised immediate supervision over subordinate photo interpreters. He recalls the following: "Actually, I thought my job as a Photo Interpreter was sort of boring and then we received the U-2 over flight film from the CIA and everything changed. I found my work much more meaningful and important. These days you can get photography like this on the internet, but back in the 50's, this was something very special, in my mind."

George J. Myers, Civilian, AFSPPF Technical Director from 1967-1976

George started out in the U.S. Navy designing torpedoes and continued to serve in the Naval Reserves. He retired at the rank of Lieutenant Commander. He worked in the civil service for 30 years at Westover AFB, MA, first with the 8th Air Force, as Chief of the Operations Analysis Division and then with AFSPPF, as Technical Director. After retiring, he worked at James River Graphics in South Hadley Falls, MA and taught computer science at Springfield Technical Community College. His motto of "Don't waste any time", led him to pursue entrepreneurial endeavors including owning a Western Auto Store and the very first Yankee Candle Shop, for three years, both in South Hadley Falls, MA. He passed away on August 27, 2012.

Allen F. Ostdiek, Capt, OIC Shipping Section from 1967-1971

Allen contributed substantially to the brainstorming sessions, during the reunion of 2012. After Allen's release from Air Force active duty in 1971, he served as publisher and editor at several rural weekly newspapers in Nebraska, for 38 years. He also became actively involved in many aspects of community life. He resigned as an EMT for the community of Lawrence, Nebraska in December 2012, after 30 years of volunteer service.

Wayne O. Smith, SMSgt, Production, Q/C and Operations from 1967-1971

Wayne served in Chem Mix, Processing, Printing, Q/C and Operations while at the facility. He was a part of the advanced cadre to Offutt AFB to relocate and integrate the AFSPPF production operation into the 544th ARTW, SAC Headquarters.

Blaine L. Thacker, Capt, Chief of Supply from 1966-1969

Blaine contributed stories of his experiences in Chapter 5. Upon leaving the Air Force, he started two IT companies and is now living full time in Costa Rica. He now raises seed capital for startup companies.

Michael L. Vergantino, SSgt, All areas of Lab Operations from 1964-1968

APPENDIX H

AFSPPF Reunion Members (As of Sept. 2013)

Name	Rank	Unit	Assignment	Years
Jack & Betty Anderson	MSgt	AFSPPF	Power Prod. Div.	1970-1974
Neal (Andy) Anderson	CMSgt	7499th Spt. Gp./497th RTG	NCOIC, Photo Ops.	1972-1980
William (Bill) & Bonnie Armstrong	SMSgt	AFSPPF	Production Div.	1969-1973
William & Josephine Bahm	CMSgt	AFSPPF	Production Div.	1972-1976
George & Ruth Baker	Lt Col	AFSPPF	Chief, Production Div.	1973-1974
Fred & Joan Battey	MAJ	6594th TS/AFSPPF	OIC, Production Div.	1963-1967
Mike & Patricia Benson	SSgt	AFSPPF	Quality Assur Div.	1971-1972
Bob & Vickie Berwaldt	MSgt	AFSPPF	Production Div.	1966-1975
Paul & Joanna Biere	Sgt	AFSPPF	Production Div.	1967-1970
James F. Blackwell	TSgt	8th RTS	Production Div.	1957-1960
		6594th TS	Production Div.	1960-1962
		7499th Spt. Gp.	Photo Ops.	1963-1966
Jerry & Mary Bohn	MSgt	7405th Spt. Sq.	Aerial Photo	1967-1970
Ron & Emmy Bonja	SSgt	AFSPPF	Production Div.	1967-1970
Robert & Carolyn Borak	TSgt	6594th TS/AFSPPF	Production Div.	1962-1973
Ronald J. Bortner	Sgt	7499th Spt. Gp.	Photo Ops.	1956-1958
Charlie & Sally Braun	SSgt	AFSPPF	Maint. Div.	1971-1974
Wayne E. & Amy Brown	A1C	8th RTS	Tech Anal Div.	1959-1963
Bill & Lois Bruce	SSgt	AFSPPF	Special Activities	1967-1970
Jeanette Bryk – Edward deceased	TSgt	8th RTS	Special Projects	1962-1964
Richard & Geri Buckelew	CMSgt	6594th TS/AFSPPF	Civil Eng Dir.	1963-1977
William J. Bugelholl – Dorothy Deceased	SMSgt	8th RTS	Photomapping	1954-1969

Name	Rank	Unit	Assignment	Years
Arlie & Sylvia Burns	TSgt	8th RTS	Photomapping	1956
				1959-1962
				1967-1970
Cal & Anne Butt	Col	AFSPPF	Commander	1974-1976
Kevin & Lorane Carrigan	CW3	8th RTS	Photomapping	1961-1963
				1967-1969
Gary Lee & Kwi Chul Casey	SMSgt	AFSPPF	Production Div.	1966-1969
		497th RTG		1983-1986
Phil & Nona Cavanagh	MSgt	AFSPPF	Special Activities	1968-1972
Lonnie & Nancy Cavin	MSgt	AFSPPF	Tech Rpt. Div.	1970-1975
Harold & Lucy Cleet	TSgt	6594th TG	Aerial Recovery Br.	1967-1978
Lee & Lynn Colville	SSgt	6594th TS/AFSPPF	Maintenance Div.	1960-1967
Ed & Cookie Comer	CW3	6594th TS/AFSPPF	Tech Anal Div.	1962-1964
Dennis & Kay Cox	SSgt	AFSPPF	Tech Anal Div.	1970-1973
Allen & Joyce Craley	Sgt	6594th TS/AFSPPF	Tech Anal Div.	1963-1967
Alfred & Linda Crane	Lt Col	AFSPPF	Chief, Qual Assur Br.	1967-1971
Lee & Michele Croxton	Sgt	6594th TS/AFSPPF	Tech Anal Div.	1962-1966
Janet Curtis – Frank deceased	Lt Col	6594th TS/AFSPPF	OIC, Logistics Dir.	1960-1965
Eugene & Jean Darling	A1C	8th RTS	Production Div.	1963-1967
Ron Denison	SMSgt	AFSPPF	Water/Waste Div.	1970-1977
Bill & Ina Dishon	SMSgt	6594th TS/AFSPPF	Production Div.	1963-1966
Don & Carol Durand	GS-15	AFSPPF	Program Support.	1963-1976

Name	Rank	Unit	Position	Years
Herbert & Joan Duval	Lt Col	8th RTS	Chief, Evaluation Dir.	1957-1960
		6594th TS/AFSPPF	Chief, Evaluation Dir.	1964-1975
Bob & Jackie Ericson, Jr.	Capt	7499th Spt. Gp.	OIC, Photo Ops.	1970-1975
Ron & Linda Erwi	SSgt	AFSPPF	Production Div.	1970-1972
Lou & Lavonne Falconieri	Lt Col	AFSPPF	Chief, Production Div.	1964-1969
Raymond & Judy Ferland	TSgt	AFSPPF	OPS Div.	1970-1974
Robert & Colleen Finnegan	Sgt	6594th TS/AFSPPF	Production Div.	1963-1966
James (Jim) & Sachiko Flaherty	CMSgt	8th RTS	Photomapping	1966-1971
Glenn & Diane Fraley	Sgt	AFSPPF	Qual Assur Div.	1973-1976
William & Sue Germer	Sgt	497th RTG	Research/Production	1987-1991
Roger & Sandra Glascock	SSgt	6594th TS/AFSPPF	Production Div..	1962-1966
Hal & Martha Gordon	Col	AFSPPF	Deputy Chief, Tech Anal Div.	1969-1973
Frank & Jane Graham	MSgt	7499th Spt. Gp.	Photo Ops.	1969-1972
John & Eve Graham	Civilian	AFSPPF	Program Support	1961-1977
Jim & Pat Grimm	CMSgt	6594th TS/AFSPPF	NCOIC, Production Div.	1963-1967
		7499th Spt. Gp.	NCOIC, Photo Ops.	1967-1972
Richard D. & Sally Hale	Capt	AFSPPF	R&D Dir.	1966-1969
Ralph & Hilda Hall	CMSgt	AFSPPF	Maint. Div.	1965-1969
Morris & Carol Halvorson	Sgt	6594th TS/AFSPPF	Production Div.	1964-1966
Bill & Jean Happel	Sgt	AFSPPF	Tech. Anal. Div.	1963-1966
Natalie Harman (deceased)	Civ/Secretary	6594th TS/AFSPPF	R&D	1960's

Name	Rank	Unit	Assignment	Years
Helen Harris – Lynn (Ed) deceased	MSgt	6594th TS/AFSPPF	Maint. Div.	1962-1967
John & Jan Hilten	Capt	7499th Spt. Gp.	Photo Ops.	1972-1976
Larry E. & Inge Hornsby	CMSgt	6594th TS/AFSPPF	Tech. Anal. Div.	1961-1965
		497th RTG	Photomapping	1956-1960
				1968-1969
Graydon & Bev Hudspeth	Capt	AFSPPF	Shift OIC, Prod Div.	1962-1967
Larry W. Isenhour	Lt Col	6594th TS/AFSPPF	Tech. Anal. Div.	1962-1964
Bob & Marilyn Jewell	MSgt	AFSPPF	Tech. Anal. Div.	1972-1975
Cheryl Johnson – Douglas deceased	Capt	6594th TS/AFSPPF	Chief, Production Br.	1963-1968
Erich D. & Judith Kassler	TSgt	497th RTG	Tech. Anal. Div.	1956-1960
Jack & Marge Klecker	SMSgt	AFSPPF	Special Activities	1972-1974
Darrell & Vera Krause	A1C	6594th TS/AFSPPF	Tech. Anal. Div.	1963-1967
Joseph & Delores LaFrance	CMSgt	AFSPPF	Admin. Office	1974-1976
Richard E. Lally	MSgt	AFSPPF	Tech. Anal. Div.	1972-1975
Joseph & Mary Laurendi	MSgt	6594th TS/AFSPPF	Test & Eval Div.	1963-1967
Henry & Barbara Leighow	TSgt	AFSPPF	OPS Div.	1971-1976
Joe & Tonny Lenihan	Sgt	7499th Spt. Gp.	Photo Ops.	1958-1961
Carl & Barb Lind	MSgt	6594th TS/AFSPPF	Production Div.	1961-1965
Robert & Patricia Marquis	MSgt	6594th TS/AFSPPF	Tech Anal Div.	1963-1973
		8th RTS	Special Projects	1955-1963
		497th RTG	Photo Ops.	1963-1966
Jack L. Martell	Capt	6594th TS	Maint. Div.	1962-1964
Patrick & Patricia Mastery	SSgt	AFSPPF	Production Div.	1970-1973

Name	Rank	Unit	Assignment	Years
Vickie Mathews – Larry deceased	MSgt	AFSPPF	Production Div.	1968-1974
		497th RTG	Photo Ops.	1974-1976
Leman & Alma McBrayer	TSgt	6594th TS/AFSPPF	Production Div.	1962-1971
Samuel D. McCulloch – Anita deceased	Lt Col	6594th TS/AFSPPF	Eval Dir.	1962-1965
James E. & Nancy McLaurin	MSgt	AFSPPF	Production Div.	1971-1974
Bruce & Linda Merritt	Sgt	AFSPPF	Production Div.	1970-1973
Betty Miller – Leroy (Moose) deceased	SMSgt	8th RTS	Special Projects	1957-1960
		6594th TS/AFSPPF	R&D Dir.	1961-1972
Donald & Barbara Miner	Sgt	8th RTS/6594th TS	Production Div.	1959-1962
John & Elizabeth Moore	CMSgt	6594th TS/AFSPPF	Production Div.	1963-1974
Thomas & Barbara Moorman	Gen	497th RTG/AFSPPF	Executive Officer	1967-1974
Willi & Annie Muller	MSgt	7499th Spt. Gp./	Photo Ops.	1967-1974
		497th RTG		1974-1978
Barney Ohare	Lt Col	7405th Spt. Sq ./7499th Spt Gp	Avionics Maint.	1966-1969
Ron & Paula Ohlmeyer		8th RTS/6594th TS/	Commander	1957-1968
For Harold Z. Ohlmeyer deceased	Col	AFSPPF		
Allen & Nancy Ostdiek	Capt	AFSPPF	Special Activities	1967-1971
Bennie & Mary Parsley	MSgt	6594th TS/AFSPPF	Production Div.	1961-1967
William & Colleen Penn	TSgt	AFSPPF	Production Div.	1969-1973
Don & Sally Porter	Capt	8th RTS	Planning	1967-1969
Joe & Evelyn Powers	MSgt	8th RTS	Tech Anal	1958-1962
Gordon Pritchard - Nicci deceased	MSgt	6594th TS/AFSPPF	Production Div.	1962-1967

Name	Rank	Unit	Division	Years
William C. Ray – Norma deceased	CMSgt	6594th TS/AFSPPF	Production Div.	1961-1971
Richard L. Revette	MSgt	7499th Spt. Gp.	Program Spt.	1970-1972
Mike & Betty Riley	Lt Col	8th RTS	Base Photo Lab	1966-1968
		AFSPPF	R&D Directorate	1969-1974
			Exec/Special Activities	1974-1976
Arthur & Mary Roberts	SSgt	6594th TS/AFSPPF	Production Div.	1964-1968
Loomis & Betty Robertson	CMSgt	7499th Spt. Gp.	Program Spt.	1970-1972
Rick & Melissa Rowles	Sgt	AFSPPF	Production Div.	1963-1965
Dennis & Georgia Sage	MSgt	AFSPPF	Production Div.	1968-1972
Russell & Rose Sanner	TSgt	6594th TS /AFSPPF	Production Div.	1961-1966
Paul & Barbara Schoen	SMSgt	AFSPPF	Production Div.	1971-1977
Lee Schram	TSgt	AFSPPF	Production Div.	1972-1976
Raymond (Dick) & Anne Schroeder	SMSgt	6594th TS /AFSPPF	Production Div.	1964-1969
Eugene & Maureen Schwenk	Sgt	AFSPPF	Maint. Div.	1967-1970
Allen (Scotty) & Pat Scott	MSgt	6594th TS /AFSPPF	R&D Dir.	1963-1973
		7499th Spt Gp/497th RTG	Photo Ops.	1973-1979
Tom & Marie Shacklett – Tom deceased	CMSgt	6594th TS/AFSPPF	Operations Div.	1964-1974
Mike & Linda Shields	SSgt	AFSPPF	Production Div.	1968-1972
William & Becky Shives	MSgt	497th RTG	Reproduction	1952-1955
Robert & Janet Sisson	TSgt	AFSPPF	Utilities Div.	1972-1976
Stephen & Diane Smith	Sgt	8th RTS	Photo Ops.	1967-1970
Wayne Smith – Sandy deceased	SMSgt	AFSPPF	Operations Div.	1967-1971
				1973-1976

Name	Rank	Unit	Assignment	Years
Lloyd & Mary Spanberger	Capt	AFSPPF	R&D Dir.	1966-1968
George & Terry Stancil	MSgt	6594th TS/AFSPPF	Maint. Div.	1963-1968
Stan & Paula Stanley	Col	AFSPPF	Vice Comdr.	1970-1974
James & Barbara Stepnowski	Capt	AFSPPF	Production Div.	1971-1974
Doc & Lucy Takeda	CMSgt	7499th Spt. Gp.	NCOIC, Spec Ops	1963-1967
		AFSPPF	R&D Dir.	1967-1971
Robert Tarkington	Sgt	AFSPPF	Supply Div.	1971-1974
Dick & Gini Temple	SSgt	8th RTS	Photomapping	1967-1970
Blaine L. Thacker	Capt	AFSPPF	Chief, Supply Div.	1966-1970
Pete & Sutin Thorpe	MSgt	8th RTS	Special Projects	1956-1961
		6594th TS/ AFSPPF	Production Div.	1961-1967
Robert & Mary Tschacher	CMSgt	AFSPPF	R&D Dir.	1972-1976
Bill Tulloch	Sgt	AFSPPF	Special Activities	1966-1970
Michael & Susan Vergantino	SSgt	6594th TS/AFSPPF	Production Div.	1960-1964
		6594th TS/AFSPPF	Production Div.	1964-1968
John & Alice Vooris	MSgt	7499th Spt. Gp.		1970-1972
		6594th TS/AFSPPF	Admin Office	1963-1967
		AFSPPF		1970-1974
Dick & Betty Wagner	SMSgt	6594th TS/AFSPPF	Production Div.	1964-1968
Suzanne Wagner – Richard (Ric) deceased	TSgt	6594th TS/AFSPPF	Maint. Div.	1963-1967
Jim & Connie Weinert	MSgt	6594th TS/AFSPPF	Tech. Anal. Div.	1963-1967
		AFSPPF		1971-1974

Name	Rank	Unit	Division	Years
George White	TSgt	8th RTS	Production Div.	1955-1960
		6594th TS/AFSPPF		1961-1968
Al & Lu Whitmore	SMSgt	AFSPPF	Eval Dir.	1972-1977
William Wood - Sarah deceased	MSgt	497th RTG	Production Div.	1960-1964
Alan Zanuccoli & Maureen Dunn	Sgt	6594th TS/AFSPPF	Production Div.	1963-1966

About the Author

Lloyd R. Spanberger (Photo by Mary L. Spanberger)

Lloyd R. Spanberger is a former U.S. Air Force Captain, who served as a research physicist while stationed at Wright Patterson AFB (WPAFB), Dayton, Ohio in the Infrared Reconnaissance Division and, later, at Westover AFB (WAFB), Chicopee, Mass in the AFSPPF. While at WPAFB, he ran a successful three-year development and test project on the X-15 rocket plane to solve problems related to the development of scanning infrared reconnaissance systems in high performance aircraft, such as the SR-71. Concurrently, he spent considerable time working to help make FLIR (Forward-looking infrared) systems operational in more conventional tactical and strategic aircraft. He was, subsequently assigned to WAFB, where his problem solving responsibilities extended over to the various image processing and analysis aspects of the satellite reconnaissance mission of AFSPPF. While assigned to the R&D directorate, he was involved with virtually all Film Return Spy Satellites our country developed. He spent over two years recalling his own personal experiences and extracting recollections from the various surviving members of the AFSPPF. The result is the writing of this book. Lloyd is now retired in Maryland.

CPSIA information can be obtained
at www.ICGtesting.com
Printed in the USA
BVHW071728180419
545903BV00001B/93/P